THE A-Z OF CURIOUS NORTHERN IRELAND

STRANGE STORIES OF MYSTERIES, CRIMES AND ECCENTRICS

DOREEN McBRIDE

The History Press

Dedicated to my husband George, who never promised me a rose garden, yet what he gave me was so much better.

First published 2025

The History Press
97 St George's Place, Cheltenham,
Gloucestershire, GL50 3QB
www.thehistorypress.co.uk

British Library Cataloguing in Publication Data.
A catalogue record for this book is available from the British Library.

978 1 80399 314 0

Typesetting and origination by The History Press.
Printed and bound in Great Britain by TJ Books Limited, Padstow, Cornwall.

Acknowledgements

Thanks are due to my late husband, George, who keeps me going and to whom this book is dedicated. I am very grateful to my cousin Vernon Finlay, who read my manuscript and corrected my many typos. His help is invaluable. He is invariably encouraging, honest and wise, and I'm very grateful to him. I am also grateful to the following for supplying me with information: Anne McMaster, Florence Chambers, the late Mrs Harry McCourt, Vicki Herbert, Richard Watson, Michell Shannon, Dr Barbara Erwin, the late Dr David Erwin, Dr Robert Logan, Jayne Adair, Maebh O'Regan, the late John Campbell, Noelle and the late Graham Millar, Aidan Campbell, Joe McLaren, Liam McElhinney, Renee Therriault, Kevin Woods – the Leprechaun Whisperer, Jack Johnston, Patrick Greer, Mairéad O'Dolan, Rosana Trainor, Dr Willim Rolston and the late Pat Cassidy, who made me laugh so hard I nearly split my sides.

I am also indebted to Jamie Clarke, Larne Museum, Marble Arch Caves, Belfast Zoo, Holywood Arches Library, Banbridge Library, Newry Library and the Linen Hall Library as well as my wonderful editors, Nicola Guy and Ele Palmer.

Introduction

I once had an American guest who said, 'Northern Ireland is a very endearing place.' I agree with her. I was born here and love it. It's full of curious things. Every rock, every stick, every stone, every hill and every mountain tell a story forming the basis of a strong storytelling tradition. The four great cycles of traditional folk tales, the Ulster Cycle, the Mythological Cycle, the Fenian Cycle and the Historical Cycle, originated in Ulster. (Northern Ireland contains six of the nine counties of Ulster and some parts of the cycles stretch across the border.) St Patrick himself spent most of his time in Northern Ireland, which contains his two major churches – Down Cathedral in Downpatrick, where the saint is buried, and Armagh Cathedral, which is the ecclesiastical centre of Ireland.

The scenery is stunning, the people friendly, humorous and helpful. I am very grateful to those who took time to craic with me. I couldn't have written this without them.

A

AMANDA MCKITTRICK ROS

The world's worst novelist, Amanda McKittrick Ros, was convinced she was a literary genius! She was born on 8 December 1860 in a house called Riverside, at Drumaness, near Ballynahinch, County Down. She was christened Anna Margaret at Third Ballynahinch Presbyterian Church on 27 January 1861, the fourth daughter of Eliza Black and Edward Amlave McKittrick, principal of Drumaness School.

She trained as a teacher in Marlborough Training College, Dublin. Her first job as was in Millbrook School, Larne, County Antrim. There she met her first husband, Andy Ross, Larne Railway Station's station master, a highly regarded position. She determined to marry him and did so on 30 August 1887. His job was well paid, which must have added to his attraction because she wrote:

> Love is pleasing – more so money,
> Powerful factor – life's best honey,
> Super for the gift of God
> To a world of sin and fraud.

Amanda's parents christened her Anna Margaret. She didn't like her given name and changed it to Amanda Malvina Fitzalan Anna Margaret McClelland McKitterick Ros, which, she said, was a much more suitable handle for a genius, a poetess with novels published and royal blood flowing in her veins. She considered 'Ros', with one 's', much more elegant than her husband's surname, 'Ross'.

Amanda's the quare geg.

Amanda's marriage appears to have been happy. As a tenth wedding anniversary present, her husband paid for the publication of the first of her 'great' novels, *Irene Iddlesleigh*. She wrote two books of poetry, *Fumes of Formation* and *Poems of Puncture*, as well as her novels. They all began as private publications because she didn't approve of traditional publishers. She said, 'They want to butter the bannock on both sides and wouldn't even let you smell the treacle!' And as for other authors, she was firmly of the opinion that their work was rubbish! The only one she admired was Marie Corelli, who some consider to be a contender for the position of the world's worst novelist! Regarding Lewis Carroll, she wrote:

> I read *Alice in Wonderland*. It's the work of a drunken bluff without one redeeming feature in its idiotic pages, written by some old clergy man in his dotage.
>
> I hear some gulled American paid over £15,000 for the original manuscript. Why has no one offered to buy my original manuscripts?

Amanda's novels are so awful they are hilariously funny, with passages such as the following:

> Sympathise with me indeed! Ah, no! Cast your sympathy on the chill waves of troubled waters, fling it on the oases of futility: dash it against the rock of gossip: or, better still, allow it to remain within the faithless bosom of buried scorn.
>
> Leave me now deceptive demon of deluded mockery, lurk no more around the vale of vanity, like a vindictive viper: strike the lyre of living deception to the strains of dull deadness, despair and doubt.

Her book caused a sensation around Ballynahinch. Miss Louie Bennet had such fun reading passages aloud to her friends that she sent a copy to Barry Pain, a popular humourist, who wrote a weekly article in a widely read magazine called *Black and White*. His review included the following comments:

> The book has not amused me. It began by doing that. Then, as its enormities went on getting more and more enormous with every line, the book seemed something Titanic, gigantic, awe-inspiring, the world is full of *Irene Iddlesleigh*, by Mrs Amanda McKittrick Ros, and I shrank from it in tears and terror.
>
> The most stupendous and monumental characteristic of it is perhaps its absence of any sense of humour.

> It was great tragedy at the price of half a crown.

Amanda was enraged and developed a lasting hatred of critics. She wrote:

> What puzzles me is why Barry Pain, that hell-deserving rodent, dared consider it his business to offer criticism without an invitation to do so? I neither sought for, nor needed his opinion. How dare he write that the monumental characteristic of my first book is its absence of any sense of humour. Humour is not a required attribute of great literature.
>
> He had no reason to shrink. Only a great writer could produce such refined words.
>
> This so-called Barry Pain, has taken upon him to criticise a work the depth of which fails to reach the solving power of his borrowed, and he'd have you to believe, varied talent. I care not for what Barry calls the book I have written. I care not for the opinion of half-starved upstarts who don the garb of shabby genteel and would feign feed the minds of the people with worthless scraps of stolen fancies.

Amanda could be very kindly, but as can be seen from the above comments, when annoyed she became vitriolic! There is a theory that Andy Ros was impotent and the spleen expressed in some of her writing is the result of sexual frustration, something no Victorian lady could ever admit to! Was that what she was confessing when she wrote:

> Within my breast I feel a flame
> That would dishonour well maintain.
> It pains me to the very heart
> Yet pleases with its deadly dart.

Amanda's book, and her reaction to criticism, caused hilarity. Undergraduate clubs were formed throughout the country, including Oxford and Cambridge. They gave prizes to the person who could read her prose without laughing for the longest period of time. Famous writers, such as Aldous Huxley and Charles Dickens, belonged to Amanda Ros clubs. Her books attracted the attention of the rich and famous. She regularly received letters from enthusiastic readers throughout the English-speaking world, who found her replies as funny as her books. Lord Beveridge, Lord Ponsonby, Lord Oxford, Sir Edward Grey and E.V. Lucas formed an Amanda Ros club in London. Robert Lynd, Sir John

Squire and Sir Desmond McCarthy visited her in Larne. She was proud of the interest shown by her aristocratic admirers, without realising they were having fun at her expense!

Critics continued to annoy her by mocking her 'great literature'. She decided they did not have sufficient intelligence to appreciate it and called them names such as, 'foul critics living off the work of those of undoubted talent', 'critic cur', 'monkey-faced morons,' 'hell-deserving rodent', 'scurrilous scribes', 'vicious vandals', 'character-clipping combination' and so on. On one occasion she wrote, 'I am the notorious boil on the tip of critics' tongues.' However, there was one critic she liked, Aldous Huxley. In 1930 she wrote to a friend saying he 'is the only critic who appears to understand my work', probably because in 1923 he began an essay, 'Euphues Redivivus', as follows:

> I have recently been fortunate in securing a copy of that very rare and precious novel, 'Delina Delaney', by Mrs Amanda McKittrick Ros, authoress of 'Irene Iddlesleigh' and 'Poems of Puncture'. Mrs Ros is a name only known to a small select band of readers. But by these few she is highly prized: one of her readers actually was at pains to make a complete manuscript of 'Delina Delaney', so great was his admiration and so hopelessly out of print the book. Let me recommend Mrs Ros's masterpiece to the attention of enterprising publishers.

Extract from *Delina Delaney*:

> A panic swept over the entire court, whilst Delina fell heavily against the front of the dock. Ladies became hysterical, some fainting, others weeping copiously, and nothing was heard save sobbing and wailing. One young girl named Fanny Fowler, who had been a companion of Delina's at school, died of shock. The sight was one never, never to be forgotten. Mothers wringing their hands in deep and groaning agony, ladies supported in the arms of their husbands: and girls screaming because their parents could not be quieted.

Unfortunately Amanda's husband dropped dead in 1917. He'd just finished eating a hearty meal that she'd cooked. She was devastated and comforted herself by saying, 'At least he died on a full stomach.' She treasured a pod taken from the peas she'd shelled for his last meal.

Andy Ross was respected and well liked, so the world and his wife turned up for his funeral. Amanda wanted to be alone with what she described as her 'great grief'. She wanted everyone to go home. She didn't appreciate all the floral

'I'm embarrassed! Amanda makes a monkey of me.'

tributes sent to her. If she didn't like the sender, she had the flowers returned in a wheel barrel! She was particularly nasty to the railway company as she felt they'd overworked Andy for years. Their funeral wreath was sent back with a note saying, 'Keep it for your own director.' He was very ill!

It was traditional for male mourners to walk solemnly after the hearse. She didn't want that so ordered the funeral director to make his horses take off at a trot the minute Andy's body was placed in the hearse. The mourners had a choice. They could either run after the hearse with their top hats and coat tails flapping, or go home! Most of them went home!

She, like most Victorians, was obsessed with death. When Barry Pain (who she described as 'Pain by name and pain by nature') died, she took great delight in writing the following epitaph for him:

Epitaph Suitable for a Critic's Tomb
My! What a bubbly, vapoury box of vanity!
A litter of worms, a relic of humanity,
Once a plaster cast of mud, a puff of breath as well.
Before you chance to wonder – remember there's a hell!
So here lies an honest critic and I tell thee what,
'Tis a thing for all the world to wonder at!

Amanda expressed her obsession with death as follows: 'We all end up as dust. DUST! I do not relish the thought. If there was any justice those possessing a superior intellect, such as mine, should return at least to pebbles, not dust!' and expressed her thoughts in what she felt was poetry!

My death robe be to me a wrap
Nothing but worms and damp can snap.
All things appear to me as nought
When in the grave we lie and rot.

A visit to Westminster Abbey inspired her to what she considered to be great poetical heights and she wrote:

Westminster Abbey
Holy Moses! Have a look!
Flesh decayed in every nook!
Some rare bits of brain lie here
Mortal loads of beef and beer,
Some of whom are turned to dust.

She ended her 'poem' with the following verse.

Famous some were – yet they died;
Statesmen – Rogues beside,
Kings – Queens, all of them do rot,
What about them? Now – they're not!

Amanda had a highly litigious nature, which resulted in her taking to the law and ending up in court. That was, and is, a very expensive course of action, so she eventually became penniless. Once, when the judge asked her a question and when she tried to answer it, she recorded:

> The poisonous ape of a barrister, that hog-washing hooligan, said such a stupid embarrassing thing I told him not to interrupt a lady when she was speaking and lifted my stick pretending I was going to hit him to teach him a lesson. If I did use filthy language ten years ago, what of it? I am not the only person to have done so and will not be the last! What about the world's so called genius Robbie Burns? Have any of the learned dignitaries at Belfast Assizes read any of his filthy productions?
>
> I quote,
>
> 'My name is Bobby Burns,
> I'm the pier of Leith.'
>
> 'The pier of Leith' How shocking! I quote, 'the pier of Leith'. How dare he be so coarse as to mention bodily functions?
>
> And what about Lord Bryon in Lalla Rookh? Filth! Sheer filth!
>
> I don't think I'm committing an act of sacrilege by saying these world-famed figures are not only guilty of using foul language in camera, as I did, but they did not hesitate to put such language in print to be handed down and pervert as yet unborn generations to behave and I, I was asked to leave the witness box.
>
> Oh, the injustice of it all! The law's an ass.

Amanda's experience with the law left her with a deep and abiding hatred of solicitors alongside her hatred of critics. She called them, among other things, 'those worms', 'those evil-minded snapshots of spleen', 'those public character tearers', 'that mushroom class of idiotics'.

Name calling didn't satisfy her spite, so before she lost her money and couldn't afford her pony and trap, she used to be driven into Larne to Cross Street on market day. There she glared into the windows of the solicitors she referred to as 'Mickey Monkey McBlear and Jamie Jarr' in their 'penurious premises', shouted insults, blew raspberries through their windows and played a toy trumpet in a threatening fashion! People used to come over from Scotland on market day. The streets were crowded and her actions caused traffic jams that had to be cleared by the police. While waiting in the traffic jam she'd caused, she took the opportunity to tell the assembled crowd how badly she felt she'd been treated. She became a tourist attraction, with people coming from Scotland to see her shenanigans.

Once, when I was giving a talk in the Larne Museum, I met the daughter of one of the solicitors, who told me her father said Amanda was an intimidating sight. Another woman said her grandfather had been taught by Amanda. He said all her pupils loved her, and that she was very beautiful and a brilliant teacher.

Her court appearances caused Amanda to become impoverished. She had to let all her servants go and rent part of her house out as a shop. That really annoyed her because her tenant refused to shut the shop on the Sabbath. She had a hand bell, which she rang demanding he close the shop, but the tenant took no notice. He also took no notice when she wrote to a letter of complaint to the *Larne Times*. He said there was nothing in his lease stipulating the hours or days on which he could open or close his shop, so there was nothing she could do. Nothing! She became so tired, so world weary, so exhausted she decided to take the waters of the spa near Ballynahinch and her old childhood home in County Down. There she met a wealthy farmer called Thomas Rogers (1857/58–1933), married him in 1922, settled down and stopped writing!

AMERICAN PRESIDENTS WITH NORTHERN IRELAND ANCESTRY

At least seventeen American Presidents claim to have Ulster/Scots ancestry. I haven't included them all because some connections appear very tenuous.

Andrew Jackson, seventh President (1829–37), said, 'I was born somewhere between Carrickfergus and the United States.' His father, also called Andrew, farmed for some time around the Castlereigh area of County Down before moving to Boneybefore, near Carrickfergus in County Antrim. He became dissatisfied with his life because no matter how hard he worked, he made a poor living. He decided to emigrate to North Carolina in search of a new life. He was accompanied by his wife, Elizabeth, their two sons, Robert and Hugh, and his father, who was also called Hugh. He died less than two years later, five days after the birth of his third son, Andrew, the future President.

Andrew Jackson's ancestral home in Boneybefore was about a mile north of Carrickfergus's thirteenth-century Norman castle. Unfortunately, it was demolished in 1860 to clear the way for the old LMS railway line to be laid

President Andrew Jackson's homestead.

between Belfast and Larne. Stones from the old cottage were used to reconstruct a new one beside the railway line, which is open to visitors. It's been renovated and furnished to show the lifestyle of the ancestral Jacksons.

James Knox Polk, eleventh President (1845–49), has ancestry that can be traced back to the north of Ireland. The exact location of his homestead has not been established but there are family links with Bloomfield Castle, near Londonderry. The surname changed to Pollock, then Polk sometime between 1672 and 1687. Captain Robert Bruce Polk emigrated from Northern Ireland along with his wife, six daughters and two sons, and settled in Somerset County, Maryland. He became the great-great-great-grandfather of the eleventh President.

Andrew Johnson, seventeenth President (1857-69). It is believed that President Andrew Johnson's family were small farmers from the Mounthill district near Larne in County Antrim. His grandfather was very young when he married and moved to Ballyeaston, near Ballyclare, County Antrim. It was from here that he emigrated around 1750. He settled in Lancaster Country, Pennsylvania, before moving to Raleigh, North Carolina, and it was here that his grandson, Andrew Johnson, the seventeenth President, was born in 1808.

Ulysses Simpson Grant, eighteenth President (1869–77), has an ancestral homestead at Dergina, near Ballygawley, County Tyrone, which can be visited. When I first visited years ago it was occupied by Nurse Isobel Simpson. She was directly descended from the President's mother, Hannah Simpson. She was a retired nurse, a delightful woman who appeared amused that she had such an illustrious ancestor! Hannah Simpson was the daughter of John and Rebecca Weir Simpson and granddaughter of John Simpson. He was born at Dergina in 1738 and emigrated to America sometime between 1760 and 1763. He settled at Horsham township, Montgomery Country, Pennsylvania, and died in 1804.

Chester Alan Arthur, twenty-first President (1881–85), came from the Dreen (or Draen), Gourley's Hill, Cullybackey, near Ballymena in County Antrim. It is a restored single-storey cottage that has been furnished in the style of the period and first opened to the public in 1968. It's a short walk from Cullybackey in a breathtaking situation overlooking the River Maines valley and it's open to the public. The President's grandfather, Alan Arthur, emigrated from here in 1816 along with his wife and son, William. Unlike some of the other Presidents' families, the Arthurs were comparatively wealthy because William, who became the President's father, was able to attend Belfast College before he emigrated at the age of 18.

Stephen Grover Cleveland, twenty-second President (1885-89) and twenty-fourth President (1893-97). (According to a State Department ruling he can be counted twice because his terms of office were not consecutive.) President Cleveland's mother was Ann Neal, the daughter of Aber Neal, a merchant. They lived in County Antrim, where his daughter Ann was born. The exact location has not been established. Aber Neal emigrated late in the eighteenth century because his politics could have had repercussions such as him being sent for trial and, if found guilty, severely fined, jailed, sold as a slave, hanged or burnt at the stake!

Aber Neal set up a publishing company in America. He was very successful, publishing and selling law books. His daughter Ann married a clergyman, Richard Falley Cleveland. Their fifth child and future President was born on 18 March 1837.

Benjamin Harrison, twenty-third President (1889–93). The exact location of his ancestral home in County Antrim hasn't been established. His great-grandfather, Benjamin Harrison, after whom he was christened, was one of the signatories of the Declaration of American Independence.

William McKinley, twenty-fifth President (1897-1901). The old McKinley homestead is on the family farm at Conagher, Dervock, close to the River Bush. The earliest member of the family to emigrate was James McKinley in 1743. He was the President's great-great-grandfather. Francis McKinley was the last member of the family to live there. He emigrated to the United States in about 1836. The McKinleys must have made a strong impression on the local population as the old homestead is still called 'McKinley's Farm'. The original dwelling is now used as a barn, a new home having been built beside it. Ireland has a tradition of not knocking old homesteads down because of a belief that the old people, that is, ancestors who once lived in the house, come at night when everyone is asleep and sit round the fire. If the house wasn't there they wouldn't know where to go and could haunt the family. That belief is dying, although there are still many ruined farmsteads present in the countryside.

President McKinley was one of four American Presidents to be assassinated. He was shot twice in the stomach by an anarchist, Leon Czolgosz, on 9 June 1901. He developed gangrene in his wounds and died on 14 September. The President was six months into his second term of office at the time and was visiting the

Pan-American Exposition in the Temple of Music in Buffalo, New York State. He liked meeting members of the public, ignored security advice and was shaking hands with a member of the public when he was shot.

Theodore Roosevelt, twenty-sixth President (1901–04). The exact location of President Roosevelt's ancestral home has not been located, although it is thought to be in Gleno, near Larne.

Woodrow Wilson, twenty-eighth President (1913-21). His ancestral home is in Dergalt, 3 miles from Strabane in County Tyrone. He is considered to be one of the most outstanding Presidents the United States has ever had. He was the grandson of James Wilson, who emigrated from County Tyrone to America in 1807. On the emigrant voyage he met Annie Adams from Sion Mills, also in County Tyrone, and the young couple married shortly after they landed in America. Their son, Revd Joseph Ruggles Wilson, was his father. Woodrow Wilson was born in Virginia. His father was one of the founders of America's Presbyterian Church in 1861. He was very proud of his Ulster-Scots (Scots-Irish) ancestry and visited his ancestral home, near Strabane, during the summer of 1899 to carry out family research. In an address at an annual banquet to a New England Society in Brooklyn on 21 December 1896, he said:

> I am not of your blood. I am not a Virginian Cavalier. But I come from blood as good as yours – in some respects better, because the Scots-Irish, although they are as much in earnest as you, have a little bit more gaiety and elasticity than you have. We believe as sincerely as you do that we really made this country.

Woodrow Wilson had a brilliant academic career before he was elected President in 1913. He is the only President to have been awarded a doctorate (a PhD in political science), so he was well able to oversee legislation, including the women's right to vote. He guided America throughout the First World War and was awarded a Nobel Peace Prize in 1919. His ancestral home is in the care of the Ulster American Folk Park. It isn't always open, but tourists can peer in the windows, read the interesting noticeboards describing its significance and history and admire the magnificent scenery. I visited it shortly after it opened and met his relatives, an elderly brother and sister. The place was delightful, with chickens walking around the yard, a turf fire and a cosy atmosphere. I was invited to have a seat by the fire and I asked what they felt about discovering they had an illustrious ancestor. They told me it was a shock! They had lived quietly, travelling no further than Plumbridge (about 9 miles away), and now they were inundated with strangers. Most visitors were very nice, some were condescending about their lifestyle and some people were downright rude. The money they earned made life a lot easier because they no longer had to worry about making the farm economic, but in some ways they would have liked to go back to their old, quiet, contented life when the height of excitement was to cycle up to the Plum (Plumbridge).

Bill Clinton, forty-second President (1993-2001). There is no proof of Bill Clinton's ancestry. He claims to be descended from Northern Irish stock. The local oral tradition records President Clinton's ancestral home as being in Roscrea, County Fermanagh, so what he says connects with the local tradition. His mother's maiden name was 'Cassidy', a common surname in County Fermanagh, so I've included him. He was the first serving president to visit Northern Ireland and has done so on several occasions. He was instrumental in drawing up the Peace Process, known as the Good Friday Agreement. He's very popular in Northern Ireland. Locals were delighted when he went shopping on Belfast's Shankill Road and insisted on paying for what he bought. He visited Omagh and talked to survivors and victims of the Omagh Bombing (1998). Twenty-nine people were killed and 300 were injured. He was visibly moved by the stories he heard.

Bill Clinton's wife, Hillary, became Chancellor of Queen's University Belfast in 2020. She is the first woman to hold that post and will do so for five years. At the time she said, 'It's my great privilege to become Queen's first female chancellor. It's a place I have great fondness for and have grown a strong relationship with over the years, and I'm proud to be an ambassador for its excellence.' Locally, the vast majority of people are delighted she accepted the post, which was reported as a coup for Queen's.

ARMADA

Girona, one of the ships in the Spanish Armada, carrying fabulous wealth and 1,300 sailors, sank off the coast of County Antrim in 1588.

Spain was determined to invade England, remove Queen Elizabeth I from the throne and put King Philip II of Spain on it. He claimed to be the rightful ruler because he'd been married to her sister, Queen Mary. He sent out an Armada of ships in May 1588 and was defeated by the English navy for three reasons: its ships were smaller and more manoeuvrable than the ungainly Spanish galleons, the weather was atrocious, and King Philip acted stupidly. He put the Duke of Medina Sidonia, an aristocrat without any naval experience, in charge of the fleet, with instructions to link up with the Duke of Parma in Flanders, with an invasion force to attack England.

King Philip was an ardent Catholic. His wife, Queen Mary, burnt so many Protestants at the stake she became known as 'Bloody Mary'. Queen Elizabeth was a Protestant, who turned England into a Protestant State. King Philip wanted to reinstate Catholicism as England's religion and stop British and Dutch privateers plundering his interests in the New World. His invasion force was thought to be invincible. The tall, stately, well-armed galleons looked impressive. However, the small, fast manoeuvrable English ships sailed between them and set them on fire. The big ships were like sitting ducks. They tried to escape by scattering up the east coast of England and around the north of Scotland. There was a howling gale. Many of the galleons perished, blown on to rocks and headlands or sunk by the weather.

Girona survived the storm, but its rudder was damaged. It limped into Killybegs in County Donegal and was patched up before setting sail round the north coast of Ireland. It was carrying survivors from three other Spanish ships as well as its own crew. There were an estimated 1,300 on board a ship designed for 400, as well as all kinds of treasure. It foundered on rocks at Portballintrae in County Antrim, which is near Dunluce Castle. There were only nine survivors. Sorley Boy McDonnell, the owner of Dunluce Castle, looked after them and gave 260 bodies found in the vicinity a decent Christian burial in nearby St Cuthbert's graveyard. Most of the remaining bodies were not recovered but one washed up on the shore at Ballygally. It was buried in an unmarked grave in the churchyard surrounding St Peter's Anglican Church, Cairncastle. In his pocket the sailor had a sweet chestnut tree seed, which were supposed to keep their owners from drowning. It germinated and grew into a huge tree that flourished until 2020, when it blew down in a storm. The trunk was removed. Locals have preserved the wood and intend to have it made into some kind of commemoration. The massive

Cairncastle Church.

root survives and is growing shoots. Sweet chestnut trees are not indigenous to Ireland but over the years seeds from that tree have been grown locally, so the Spanish Armada has had a direct effect on the north of Ireland.

Over the years many divers set out to find *Girona*'s treasure. They studied records of winds and tides but failed to locate the ship. Eventually a Belgium crew, led by Robert Stenuit, an experienced diver, found *Girona* on 27 June 1967 at Port na Spaniagh. Stenuit's approach differed from other attempts. He asked the locals where *Girona* was. They pointed at a rocky outcrop on the shore and told him, 'That's where it went down.' When I was a child growing up in Northern Ireland we had family outings to Portballintrae. The rocky outcrop was pointed out to us and we were told it was called Port na Spaniagh because it marked the spot where a Spanish galleon had gone down! Locals said, 'Nobody believes us when we tell them!' Stenuit was different. He stated:

> When we arrived in Portballintrae, I began my search where all the contemporary historical documents advised me to go and dive. That is just next to the Giant's Causeway. The Portballintrae locals were much interested by our activities and we soon developed very friendly ties with local amateur divers.

Girona wasn't found on the first few dives, then on 27 June 1967, approximately a year after he'd located the wreck, Stenuit reported, 'The first artefact from the *Girona* which I found was a large lead ingot, it was boat-shaped and covered with marks in Roman numerals.'

Stenuit wisely kept the knowledge of where the wreck was located secret until he had registered it properly. Eventually the treasure was passed on to Belfast's Ulster Museum, where it is on view. It's a fabulous hoard of gold jewellery and coins along with more mundane utility goods such as kitchen equipment. They give a valuable insight into how the sailors lived. As for Portballintrae, Robert Stenuit treated the village to a wake the likes of which is rarely seen. According to my friends Noelle and the late Graham Millar, who had the use of a house in Portballintrae near the Beach Hotel, it lasted a week and it took the population a long time to recover! It was in the tradition of all good wakes; a great party with mighty craic!

B

BELFAST NATURAL HISTORY AND PHILOSOPHICAL SOCIETY

Belfast Natural History and Philosophical Society is, and has been, organised by enthusiastic volunteers since its inception. It has survived for more than 200 years and is still going strong today! The society was founded by Dr James Lawson Drummond (1783–1853). He was a teacher in Belfast Academical Institution, known locally as Inst, where he gave students preparing for the Presbyterian ministry a smattering of medical knowledge, a curious task when viewed through our eyes today. In 1820 he published *Thoughts on the Study of Natural History* and that publication led to the formation of Belfast Natural History Society in 1821. Several of his old pupils, including Robert Patterson, who wrote zoology books that were used in schools throughout Ireland, were among the founding members. In 1829 a site was secured in College Square North for a museum, which was formally opened on 1 November 1831. It was the first provincial museum in Ireland and was used for educational purposes and to attract publicity. Society members provided specimens. Perhaps the most notable is Thomas Gregg's purchase of an Egyptian mummy (initially identified as Kabooti, later ammended to Takabuti) when he visited Egypt. She was unrolled on 27 January 1835 at a special meeting, during which members took notes at each successive stage. Advertisements were placed in the local press stating the unrolled Egyptian mummy could be seen at the museum on Saturday 31 January, Monday 2 February, Wednesday 4 February and Friday 6 February, after which the bandages were replaced with the exception of the head and feet. That's amazing! The general public invited to see the body of a naked woman in the Victorian age!

The society changed its name to Belfast Natural History and Philosophical Society in 1842 so it could discuss a broader range of topics. It had a tremendous influence on the development of Belfast. It helped establish the Botanic Gardens in 1827, initiated the publication of the first series of the *Ulster Journal of Archaeology* in 1853, Belfast Naturalists' Field Club in 1863 and established an Archaeological Section in 1917. The society gifted its specimens to Belfast Corporation in

Members of BNHPS at the grave of their first President, which they restored.

1910 and its books and records in 1924, thus laying the foundation for Belfast Corporation's first museum, which developed into the Ulster Museum on the Stranmillis Road, now part of the National Museums organisation. Kabooti takes pride of place, intriguing, horrifying and thrilling children!

The memory of James Lawson Drummond is lovingly preserved. He died in 1853 and was buried in Ahoghill Old Graveyard beside his third wife. Belfast Natural History and Philosophical Society hired Nathan Morrow, a stonemason from Glenarm, to renovate the old grave. Nathan has been nominated for a Heritage Angel Award. By the way, Inst was originally set up to provide education for boys from the age of 11 through university level. The university element of Inst led to the foundation of Queen's University Belfast, which opened its doors in 1847 and is now a Russell University. James Drummond was instrumental in its foundation.

BLACK PIG'S DYKE

The Black Pig's Dyke is a series of huge, mysterious double earthen banks that stretch from Counties Down and Armagh into the south of Ireland. They have a ditch between them and they run alongside some of the present-day roads. Nobody knows why they were built or what function they once served. Were parts of them flattened as farmers went about their work? Did they once form a complete structure running from the eastern shore in County Down to the west in County Fermanagh, then out of Northern Ireland to the western shore in County Donegal? Did they mark a border? Were they used as a ceremonial road, or what? Nobody knows.

There are a lot of folk tales about the Black Pig's Dyke, usually about wicked schoolmasters turning their pupils into pigs. My favourite story is set in Meigh, a small village near Newry. There's a dip in the road where a bridge crosses the River Flurry. At this point the Black Pig's Dyke looks like a hill covered in shrubs. The story says that once upon a time long, before St Patrick came to Ireland, there was a wicked schoolmaster who was a master of the Black Art, in other words he was a Devil worshipper, and an expert in performing black magic. He had a terrible temper and when he flew into a rage, he waved his magic wand and turned the whole class into hares and hounds. Then he told the hounds, who were his favourite pupils, to chase the hares. That was fun if you'd been turned into a hound and terrible if you were turned into a hare.

Michael was a small, quiet, good wee boy. The evil schoolmaster hated everything that was good, so he hated poor Michael. He turned the poor lad into a hare every day. The hounds bullied, chased and bit Michael, so he learned to dread going to school. He started waking up in the middle of the night and screaming because of nightmares about being killed by hounds. Eventually his father discovered what the schoolmaster was doing and he was *furious*! Apart from anything else, he didn't like having his sleep disturbed! He went to school, grabbed the magic wand and turned the schoolmaster into a gigantic black pig with huge tusks! That made the pupils nearly laugh their legs off. The schoolmaster was so furious he dug his tusks into the earth and used them to plough a trench right across Ireland. That trench became known as the Black Pig's Dyke.

The Black Pig.

The Dane's Cast is another name for the Black Pig's Dyke. Although flattened in some places, it can be traced across marshland such as that between Rathfriland and Poyntzpass, where gorse bushes grow along a line where the dyke would be expected to run. A theory developed during the early part of the twentieth century that Black Pig's Dyke had once formed a boundary between the north and the south and they called it the Wall of Ulidia. It was suggested that the north and south of Ireland have always differed both politically and culturally. Over time this idea has become less likely but it has inspired writers, such as W.B. Yeats (*The Valley of the Black Pig*) and James Joyce (*Finnegan's Wake*), to explore the complexity of politics in Ireland.

C

CLOUGHMORE STONE

Cloughmore Stone, known locally as 'the big stone', sits 300m (1,000ft) on Slieve Martin in the Mourne Mountains above the pretty village of Rostrevor. It's a giant granite boulder that weighs more than 50 tons, a glacial erratic, thought to have been carried over from Scotland by ice during the last Ice Age. It is sitting on Silurian metasedimentary rock, that is rock that was formed when layers of sediments, such as mud or sand, came under great pressure as more sediments landed on top so that they turned into solid rock. The Silurian is a geological time period of over 400 million years ago. It was a time of great change, including the

The Cloughmore Stone.

melting of an Ice Age. Frozen rivers are called glaciers. As the glaciers flow slowly along the gorge they take great lumps out of the landscape and can carry them far away from their original 'home', dumping them down in places that are very different from where they originated, so the Cloughmore Stone is a curious rock when compared to its surroundings.

Local legend says the giant Finn McCool, who was in the Cooley Mountains on the other side of Carlingford Lough at the time, lost the bap (became very annoyed) with a giant called Ruscaire, who he saw on the Mourne Mountains. They fought for three days and three nights until Finn picked up a huge boulder and threw it. It landed on Ruscaire's head and killed him. Today the boulder is known as the Cloughmore Stone. It sits in a breathtaking position overlooking Carlingford Lough, the Cooley Mountains and the Mournes. The area has been declared a National Nature Reserve and an Area of Special Scientific Interest. There are three marked trails. They vary in length from 1¼ miles to 4½ miles, taking the visitor through the forest. There is a car park about a fifteen-minute walk from the Cloughmore Stone. It's steep, but well worth the effort.

COTS AND COT RACING

In 1850 Henry Newland, the fishing parson from Westbourne in Sussex, described cots as follows:

> The cot is a rough sort of boat, very much in vogue on Lough Erne. The whole lake is full of islands, some of which are very large, and many cultivated, and thus the cot is as necessary to these aquatic farms as a wagon would be to a farm onshore.

Newland doesn't appear to have liked the cot's appearance because he continued:

> It is built somewhat in the form of an elongated tablespoon, with the handle off; it is of the rudest possible workmanship, frequently of unplaned planks nailed together and roughly caulked, but without the vestige of a keel.

Cots took brides to weddings and corpses to funerals as well being used for fishing and wild fowling and to move livestock between the mainland and the islands. Sometimes the animals were put into a cot and sometimes they were tied on to ropes and made to follow the cot by swimming across the water. Cots are very stable, so could be used daily when cows on an island farm needed to be milked. It was possible to take buckets of milk across the water without spilling a drop. They were once used to transport heavy materials around Lough Erne. Working cots were very different from racing cots and those in everyday use by farmers. They were larger and heavier. Some weighed somewhere between 16 and 20 tons. They usually had a mast and a sail, were fitted with four to six oars and their course was set by a paddle fixed to a pivot wheel. The largest cots were 50ft long, 10ft wide in the centre, tapered to 3ft at each end and were 5ft 6in deep. Even though they were very heavy, they had a shallow draft. Timber, iron, lead, coal and slates were imported through Ballyshannon, taken by horse and cart to Belleek and on to Enniskillen. Stone was carried from Carrickreagh quarry to Enniskillen and eels from the weirs at Killyhevlin to Belturbet. Portland stone used to build Castle Coole travelled to its destination in cots.

It used to be possible, when walking along Lough Erne's shores, to see a cot completely submerged in water, which is a unique way to preserve them.

Regular traditional cot races were held during the 1800s at Crom. Henry Newland described a cot's performance. He wrote:

> You would be surprised if you saw a Lough Erne boat-race; awkward and clumsy as it seems, if the day should happen to be perfectly still, it is the cot that invariably wins the race; their great broad flat frames seem to slip over the surface without touching it. But the slightest breeze is fatal to them; they drop to the leeward as unresistingly as a floating plank.

Lough Erne Heritage is a charitable organisation that aims to encourage local heritage research. Fred Ternan, of Lough Erne Heritage, who used to live on Inniscoornan Island (Inniscoorna means 'island of the sweet-smelling flowers'), said, 'Cots had disappeared completely from the lough. We felt that was a shame.' The Heritage Committee decided it would be a good idea to build one. At first they thought they'd make a mock-up of plywood just to show what it looked like, then they thought, 'Why don't we build the real thing?' They contacted local people, such as John Reihill, a local historian, to find out as much about cots as possible. Luckily a local schoolteacher, Miss B. Beggin, known as Detta, had done a detailed drawing of a cot in the 1950s and it was used as a plan. Detta had since married and moved to England but she visited Fermanagh and approved of what they were doing. In 2016 they organised a project, during which volunteers built two cots of the traditional length, but 2in wider than usual so they could accommodate wheelchairs.

In May 2016, Lough Erne Heritage Members decided to resurrect cot racing. Another cot was hurriedly built and finished a few days before the planned event. The first cot race for 100 years was held in August 2016 at Crom. The organisers recreated what is referred to as 'the famous cot race', which took place in 1856, at Crom. That race became famous because the crew's leader, John Goodwin, refused to take the prize money on behalf of the winning team. The team said they'd rather Lord Erne helped them arrange the return of their much-loved parish priest, Father Clarke, than win any amount of money! Father Clarke fled to America when he was warned he was going to be arrested for officiating at a mixed marriage. Lord Erne used his influence and was able to get the charges dropped. The priest returned to Fermanagh and ended his days in Newtownbutler.

The Lakeland Heritage cot race was a great success. John Goodwin's great-great-grandson, Michael Goodwin, took part in the race, while the present Lord Erne, the great-great-grandson of the 1856 Lord Erne, gave out the prizes. Participants themselves said the race itself was 'mighty craic', but the best thing was having fun together, learning new skills and developing new friendships.

CULDEES

The Culdees belonged to a very early Christian sect, formed by Joseph of Arimathaea, a very wealthy man who had been present when Jesus was crucified. He asked for permission to take the body of Jesus and intern it in an unused tomb in his own garden. He witnessed the resurrection. Folklore says he travelled to England, preached Christianity and attracted followers. Some of Joseph's followers crossed the Irish Sea and settled on Devonish Island in Lough Erne, where they became known as the Culdees (Ceile De, people of God). The Culdees' beliefs are based on Celtic spiritualism, respecting nature and placing unconditional love of God at its core. They believe that being conscious of the Great Creator will at best prevent the gradual destruction of our world and at worst make the individual happy.

The Culdees believed life is a circular journey during which we travel from God back to God. During that journey we are supposed to learn that we are fused to the Divine Spirit. They looked upon their religion as 'the people's church'. They didn't place much emphasis on a hierarchy, so when St Culmban wrote to Pope Boniface in the sixth century, he wrote as an equal, not as an inferior being. Their settlements differed from other monastic settlements in that they consisted of a series of detached huts, or beehives, rather than a large church building.

Them Culdees were great scholars.

The Culdee monks were scholarly, spending their lives gaining knowledge, making music and studying the scriptures. They travelled widely, spreading their knowledge wherever they went so that Fermanagh became known as a land of saints and scholars, a reputation that spread throughout Ireland. It is thought that St Patrick was a Culdee. There isn't any evidence showing that he visited Devonish Island, but as Lough Erne is a major highway leading to Lough Derg, which is strongly associated with him, he's almost certainly bound to have visited it.

St Augustine, the then Pope, decreed individuals should pay clergymen to pray for them. St Patrick strongly disagreed with him and so did the Culdees. They believed people were quite capable of praying for themselves. They also believed that people should be given Bibles written in their own language. It's amazing how, from the seventh century onwards, well-documented arguments between the Culdees and the Catholic Church foreshadow later Protestant–Catholic disputes that led to the establishment of Protestantism and eventually the Reformation.

The Culdees annoyed the Catholic Church because they saw no reason to pay dues to an organisation they neither respected nor paid allegiance to. That annoyed St Bernard (Pope 1090–1153) and they refused to go to confession or be married by clergy belonging to his Church. He said, 'The Culdees are beasts, absolute barbarians, a stubborn, stiff-necked and ungovernable generation, and abominable; Christian in name, but in reality pagans.'

The Culdees living around Lough Erne used to strip naked and be baptised in the River Erne, which is the second-longest river in Ulster. It flows from the north of Ireland into the south and forms part of the border between the two countries. Unfortunately the custom degenerated over time and became more of an orgy than a Christian service! Tents were erected and the indulgence of all sorts of sexual practices became commonplace.

There was great pressure on the Culdees to conform. Over time the different Christian groups combined under the Church St Peter founded in Rome and some of the Culdees did conform, while others emigrated to America.

D

DAPHNE BELL MBE AND THE ULSTER COLLEGE OF MUSIC

Daphne Bell (1926–2006) was one of the most amazing people I have ever had the privilege of counting as a friend. She was addicted to music and more or less singlehandedly gave birth to the Ulster College of Music. She acted as an Honorary Director for years. She had a profound influence on all types of music that was, and is, performed within Northern Ireland, and beyond its boundaries.

In many ways Daphne was a formidable character. She could make grown men shake within their shoes. I once found the then Principal Flute of the Ulster Orchestra hiding in a cubby hole under the stairs of the college because 'Miss Bell wants me to help carry a piano up the stairs and I've a bad back!'

Miss Bell insisted on good manners and of being addressed what she considered properly. I am proud to have gained the right to call her 'Daphne'! Mere acquaintances, or people she did not consider friends, were granted a withering stare if they dared use her Christian name. She would draw herself to her full height and width and pronounce with great dignity, 'The name is Miss Bell, if you please!' She was famous for wearing large hats and cloaks, and for her ability to make an entrance. She had a great sense of humour and was marvellous company.

Daphne was born in Dublin in 1926. Her parents were Quakers so she was sent, as a boarder, to Friend's School in Lisburn. Her father was an auctioneer. She once described how her mother was giving a tea party when her father arrived unexpectedly, lifted the silver teapot, said, 'I have a client for this,' and disappeared. Possibly being used to such unexpected

'The name's Miss Bell, if you please.'

childhood occurrences gave her the ability to cope in emergencies. She never panicked, she just dealt with the situation.

Daphne had a deep and abiding love of music. She told me she trained as a performer because she wanted to be a concert pianist. 'However,' she said:

> I could never make piano sound as I felt. I was doing my final exams when I heard the examiners talking about me. I have very acute hearing. One said to the other, 'She's terrible! She doesn't even look good, but she had gone to the trouble of learning her pieces perfectly. She has a forceful personality. She'd make a very good music teacher, so let's pass her.' That's why I became a music teacher.

Daphne taught in several schools, with her last school appointment being Ashfield Girls' Secondary School (now Ashfield Girls' High School) in East Belfast. That's where our friendship began in 1960 when I was appointed as a biology teacher. In 1966 she was appointed as a lecturer at Stranmillis Teacher Training College (now Stranmillis University College). That was her day job until she retired in 1983. In her spare time she started the Ulster College of Music, a private institution that aimed at producing excellent musical education.

One of the first things Daphne did when founding the college was to find a distinguished patron, Dame Ruth Railton, founder of the National Youth Orchestra of Great Britain. She also obtained the outstanding violinist and teacher Jaroslav Vancek. She was amazing. She managed to persuade distinguished musicians to teach in the college with no reward apart from being referred to as a 'visiting professor', a ticket either from across the Irish Sea or from the south of Ireland, accommodation in one of the college students' homes and food, limitless cups of tea of coffee and a pittance to pay them for their trouble. Parents took turns to host visiting professors, man the kitchen and make endless cups of tea or coffee for whoever required them.

Daphne organised hilarious Christmas parties for parents. All food was provided by parents, so the party didn't cost any money and the craic was mighty! Parents were allowed to wait in Daphne's study while students were having lessons. This provision, and the parties, made the college a very social, friendly place.

The college was unique because it accepted children and adults as students. Adults weren't required to pass an audition to be admitted. Desire was enough. My son, daughter, father and I went for lessons. Daphne used to boast, 'We have three generations of the same family as students and the grandfather is in his eighties!' (That was true.) Adults were slotted in with children who were of a similar standard. Generally speaking, the youngsters achieved a high standard while the adults had more enthusiasm than either talent or sense! Daphne organised two adult concerts a year where we could perform for each other, 'Adult Antics' in December and 'June Jollities' in June. They were fun. Children were strictly barred because 'they are good and we are useless' and we didn't want them to 'see us carrying on, like a pack of idiots as that would set them a bad example'! It was there I met an enthusiastic milkman who played the cello. He said he was 'the talent the world had not yet discovered', and Rosie, who played the piano beautifully, unless she knew somebody was listening when she would shake like a leaf and forget the notes. Perhaps the most memorable of all was Judge John Curran, who told me he'd rather be an opera singer than a judge! In the middle of the Troubles, he needed police protection and his presence at the college was a bit of a risk. Daphne made sure the timings of his lessons varied so the IRA could not see a pattern and murder him.

John frequently got parts in the chorus of Fitzwilliam Operatic Company. It put on excellent annual light opera productions in the Grand Opera House, Belfast. He told me how embarrassed he once was when in the middle of a dress rehearsal the police arrived, announced that they'd been told there was a bomb in the building, and ordered everyone to leave immediately. Poor John was dressed in green tights with a leather jerkin and a wig. He said he dandered round Belfast praying he didn't meet anyone he knew until the police gave him the all clear.

John's police guard attended rehearsals with him. Once one of his heavies was forced by a coach to help her demonstrate a dance. The heavy objected, but the coach was insistent and found he was such a talented dancer he was awarded a solo spot. John laughed as he said, 'I was jealous!'

I think the best way to give a flavour of the college is to describe my family experiences. My son John was enrolled as a student when he was 4 years of age. Daphne gave him a brief amusing 'game' to test his musical ability before accepting him. He left when he was 18 to read music at the University of Ulster. The college gave him a sound musical education.

'I'm the talent the world has not yet discovered!'

He started by learning the tonic sol-fa along with the other tots. When the infants had mastered what John referred to as 'hand signals', they learned how to play a recorder. You were expected to practise and to improve. If you didn't you faced an interview with Daphne, who pointed out that parents were paying for lessons and it was only fair that you make the most of the opportunity. If you weren't going to be serious you should leave the college. She maintained that, 'Children must learn that music is serious. It's fun but serious fun so they have to work hard and do exams.'

The recorder class were entered as individuals to the Associated Board's Grade 1 recorder exam. They all passed and were allowed to learn to play the piano. John's first piano teacher was Eamonn Friel. He enthused John to such an extent my daughter Leona decided she wanted to play the piano (Leona is eight years older than John). She was welcomed with open arms, although she was 16 at the time. John did the required exams until the age of 12, when he was told he was ready to learn to play an instrument. He'd always dreamed about playing the trumpet, but Daphne said, very firmly, 'John you might like another instrument more than the trumpet. Let's find out.'

Members of the Ulster Orchestra taught in the college. John was taken round and introduced to each teacher, handed an instrument, shown how to play it, then given a go at playing it himself. He tried everything available, then asked if he could try both the trumpet and the clarinet again. He wasn't quite sure which instrument he preferred. To my great relief he chose the clarinet (it's quieter than the trumpet!). Daphne had a very good relationship with the Ulster Orchestra and he enjoyed his lessons with Paul Schumann, one of the orchestra's clarinetists. The college's students, wearing their regulation uniform consisting of a blue sweater, sold programmes in return for a free ticket at Ulster Orchestra concerts. The college's orchestra practice on Saturday mornings appears to have been hilarious!

When John was 14, Daphne insisted, to his great disgust, that he audition for a place in the Ireland's National Youth Orchestra. John said very firmly he wanted to spend his summer holidays 'larking about', not spending a week preparing to give a concert in the RDS in Dublin. I couldn't help laughing because he's very competitive. He doesn't like to be beaten and the audition was a competition. He didn't know whether he should be pleased or disgusted when he gained a place! Eventually he became their Principal Clarinetist. I want to stress the standard of teaching in the Ulster College of Music was very high. Other students did as well, if not better, than John. All students were given opportunities to excel.

Daphne believed music students needed chances to perform, so she organised yearly concerts and took advantage of whatever other chances turned up. John and three other students were chosen to form a wind quartet. She convinced British Midland Airways they needed her wind quartet to help advertise their inaugural flight between Belfast and Paris.

The quartet were filmed playing their instruments in Aldergrove, boarded the flight and flew to Paris, along with a film crew, and were filmed at a couple of locations, including on the Eiffel Tower. I can only write from the point of view of my son. He had a ball. He was thrilled when he came home because, as a hungry teenager, he'd had three breakfasts: one at home, one in Aldergrove and another one in Charles de Gaulle Airport. The quartet appeared on the six o'clock and the ten o'clock news. They also broadcast, playing very badly, on Radio Ulster. Daphne asked them what happened as they'd 'fallen about'. They said one of them had a wrong note, or something. I was surprised when she said, 'Don't worry about it. These things happen sometimes and it's over and done with now.'

Eventually John went on to do a music degree at the University of Ulster. Many other college students went on to do music degrees and at least one obtained a place at Cambridge University.

I got fed up waiting for John to have his lessons. I had to travel from Banbridge to Belfast and there wasn't a lot to occupy my time in Belfast from 4 p.m. to 8 p.m. on a Tuesday evening during the Troubles. Coffee and chat in Daphne's study was fun, but four hours was a bit much! I decided to take up the piano again. My experience as an adult student in the Ulster College of Music is typical of other adults. We had more enthusiasm than talent but benefited from excellent tuition. I had enjoyed lessons as a child, but when my teacher retired my parents made no effort to find me a new one. I was so rusty I had to almost start at the beginning again. I was terrible but enjoyed my lessons with Jim Moore. He was fun and infinitely patient. After a year of being awful on the piano I thought, 'Why can't I learn to sing?' That was something I'd always wanted to do and never had the opportunity. I was really nervous when I asked Daphne! She said, 'Why not?' and arranged for a suitable tutor, the soloist Shirley McGlaughlin. I loved singing! I practised night and day, at the piano, round the house and in my car. My family unkindly said my efforts killed the cat! Shirley said, at Christmas when I'd been singing for four months, 'Doreen, you're ready do an exam. It will focus your efforts, give you something to work towards and be good for you.' I agreed to give it a go – I fully expected to be told I was doing Grade 1. Shirley asked me if I'd ever done any theory exams. I had, but didn't know where or when and my certificates had been lost over the years. 'In that case,' she said, 'you're going to have a go at Grade 5 Associated Board and do Grade 5 Theory at the same time. I'd rather put you in for Grade 6 Voice because your voice would carry you through. At Grade 5 you'll have to do sight singing and other tests you'll find a bit of a struggle because of your lack of experience. You'll be doing very well to scrape a pass, but it'll be good for you.'

I freely admit how embarrassed my son and I were to find ourselves in Mrs Friel's theory class! We sat at opposite sides of the room and didn't look at each other until I was struggling to answer a question and felt waves of sympathy coming from John. Later on he got stuck and I, in turn, felt sympathy for him. Going out the door John said, 'I didn't know …' and I said, 'Well you knew … and I didn't!' From that point on we were very supportive of each other and our relationship deepened.

Daphne said, 'Doreen, you could say we have a right cheek entering you for an exam after only eight months' singing. You're going to need all the help you can get so I've asked Elizabeth Bicker to accompany you. You'll like her.' I did! Elizabeth was a professional pianist I knew by sight. She was well known, and admired, locally. As a performer she was talented, elegant, poised, with a lovely personality. As far as I was concerned, she could not have been better. I was very nervous. She made me relax. She was fun! During the exam I was pleased with the way I performed my set pieces, made a mistake in my study, staggered through the ear tests and then came my bête noire! Sight singing! I hadn't a clue, so asked the examiner if we please could come to an arrangement about that part of the exam, so that I didn't do it and he didn't give me any marks. He refused, firmly placed a piece of music in front of me and said, 'Here, have a go at that. I'm going to give you marks for standing there!' I thought, 'I'm probably going to need them!' and started wobbling away in a pathetic attempt! When I'd finished he came over and looked at the music. 'I thought so!' he proclaimed. 'You got the last three bars exactly right, but back to front! Something must have gone in. Keep at it. It'll come.' I passed with three marks to spare!

Daphne was delighted. 'Now,' she said, 'it's time for you to start doing festival work. That should be easy for you. You're a teacher. You're used to an audience and there won't be many people there. We'll put you into Belfast Music Festival's Light Opera Class and give you Professor Geoffrey Pratley as your tutor.' I was gobsmacked! The late Professor Pratley came over from London's Royal Academy of Music to the Ulster College of Music once a fortnight. I felt very nervous meeting him because he was a well-known pianist who accompanied performers with worldwide recognition, such as Paul Tortelier and Dame Janet Baker. It was a privilege to have him as my teacher. When he was in Belfast, Geoffrey taught both the piano and singing. I was acquainted with him because John had already 'graduated' to have him as his piano teacher.

I got on by leaps and bounds with Geoffrey and was entered to sing Ivor Novello's 'First Music in May' in Belfast Music Festival. My daughter, Leona, who was training as a nurse at the time, said she'd come as support. What I didn't realise was I would be the only person of a certain age entered to sing. There were all these beautiful young girls being supported by their mothers and then there was me, supported by my daughter. It was a large audience. I nearly died! Leona and I sat near the back of the hall. I was so frightened I thought I'd have a heart attack and need to be carried out to an ambulance. I watched in horror as young woman after young woman got up and sang beautifully. At last it was my turn. I got up on the stage and began. I had to sing two verses of my song. Geoffrey had told me to sing the second verse faster than the first one. I saw the exit sign above the door and thought, 'Gee, I wish I was on the other side of that!' and raced through the last verse. When I finished and was getting down off the stage Leona caused the audience to burst out laughing because she forgot where she was, rushed up to the front of the hall, cried as she flung her arms around me and said, 'My wee Mummy! I'm so proud of you. You stood there and you sang it. You didn't forget your words or anything! You were great!' I wasn't that great. I got 72 marks, which was third from the bottom of all the marks awarded.

After that I did a lot of festival work, entering into light opera and also folk song categories. To my great amazement I won the contralto class in Portadown Festival and came home with a huge cup. There was only one person in the class and that person was me, but I got 83 marks and the adjudicator said I deserved the cup. I was delighted, although my family unkindly suggested I'd stolen it! Daphne then decided it was time I faced a 'proper' audience, so I was sent to sing at a variety of functions along with other college students. Two occasions stand out in my memory, namely when my son and I, along with about half a dozen others, were sent to a church function in Whiteabbey. I was shaking with nerves. John leaned against the wall, crossed his legs in a casual fashion and said, 'I don't know what you're worried about. As long as you don't drop dead nobody'll remember what you do!' In retrospect I think he was right but at the time dropping dead appeared to be an option! The other memorable event was in an old people's home when an old lady fell asleep during my performance and fell off her chair! I was singing 'The Garton Mother's Lullaby' at the time, so that seemed appropriate.

When John went to uni we both stopped attending the Ulster College of Music. Dad had stopped some years previously, saying he'd decided he was too old to train as a concert pianist. John works in industry but still has fun playing in a band, while I gained enough confidence to be able to incorporate singing folk songs with storytelling. I, like other students of the Ulster College of Music, will be eternally grateful to Daphne Bell and the college for what they gave me. The college would not have existed without her vision, persistence and enthusiasm.

E

ERROL FLYNN

Errol Flynn, that swashbuckling, hard-drinking, womanising Hollywood star of movies such as *Captain Blood* and *Robin Hood*, produced between 1935 and 1950, had a strong connection with Northern Ireland. His father, Theodore Thompson Flynn, was a marine biologist, who began his career in Australia, where Errol was born. Theodore was so pleased to have a son when he discovered a new type of kelpfish (kelp is a type of seaweed), he named it *gibbonsia erroli*, after his son. He was appointed Professor of Zoology to Queen's University Belfast in 1931, and remained there until he retired in 1948. He was Chief Casualty Officer for Belfast when Belfast was blitzed by Hitler during the Second World War and was awarded the OBE (Order of the British Empire) for his services in 1945.

Professor Flynn was Director of the Marine Biology Station in Portaferry, which he founded in 1936. When I was a student it was mandatory for final year Zoology students to spend two weeks there during a period of neap tides, when the tide is a little higher and a little lower than normal. The university bought the building in 1972 and it is now used for student education and as a research station. The Marine Biology Station is situated where water coming from the Arctic meets water from the tropics, resulting in an unusually diverse fauna, so it is possible to find creatures that dwell in Arctic waters alongside those from the tropics.

Professor Flynn had a large number of friends, including one who knew Michael O'Reilly, expert horseman and the owner of O'Reilly's bar in Dromara. Errol Flynn auditioned for and won a major role in a forthcoming movie, *The Charge of the Light Brigade*, provided he improve his horse-riding skills because filming the movie was going to be dangerous. That prediction proved to be true, as during filming 200 horses and one stunt man died. (In those days horses taking part in a movie were considered expendable. Animal rights and welfare has improved enormously since.) Michael O'Reilly spent some considerable time with Errol, who enjoyed his time in Dromara, improved his horse-riding skills and excelled in the movie.

Professor Flynn lived in rented accommodation on the Stranmillis Road Belfast until Errol helped him finance a Tasmanian-styled house called 'Kurrajong' at Kilclief, in a spectacular situation overlooking Strangford Lough. It was the first house he had ever owned. It looks sober and could not be more different from the house in Malibu that Errol Flynn shared with friend David Niven, which they called 'Cirrhosis-by-the-Sea'!

'You'd never believe it! When I was young Errol Flynn used to ride me!'

F

FAIRIES

Today few Irish people believe in fairies, but as strange things happen, most people, (including me) are reluctant to risk annoying them! There is no way in which I would build a house over a traditional fairy path, or cut down a fairy thorn.

According to tradition, fairies used to live in heaven with the Devil and all the little devils, God and the angels. One day a great fight broke out in heaven between God and the Devil. The fairies were delighted. They don't believe in fighting, but they love to watch a good fight and this was a real humdinger! The fairies sat on the fence, so to speak. Every time when God and the angels appeared to be winning, they shouted encouragement like 'Sock it to them God!', 'Give them what for!', 'Knock their stuffing out!', or 'Knock the melt out of them'. Whenever the Devil appeared to be winning they changed sides and shouted encouragement to him. After three days and three nights, God won and threw the Devil and the little devils out of heaven. They went to hell, which is beneath the earth, and that's where they've lived ever since. Then God turned to the fairies and said, 'You didn't join me in the fight against evil!' God looked angry and the fairies felt worried as they answered, 'No, God. We didn't. We don't believe in fighting.'

God thought for a minute then said, 'You didn't fight alongside the Devil either, did you?'

'No, God. We didn't.'

God thought for a few minutes more before saying, 'You should always fight evil. You didn't do that so you can't stay in heaven with Me and the angels. On the other hand, you didn't help the Devil so it would be wrong to send you to hell. Tell you what I'll do, I send you to earth to wait until Judgement Day, when I'll make up my mind if I'll grant you eternal life. You won't be able to die until then.' With that God threw the fairies out of heaven. They fluttered down to earth and most of them landed in Ireland.

Irish fairies are not the dainty creatures envisaged by Disney. There are many different types. The most well-known are the small ugly figures known as leprechauns. They are the only fairies to be recognised by the EU as an endangered species thanks to the efforts of Kevin Woods, the Leprechaun Whisperer. He told me, 'It took me nine years to make those foolish EU bureaucrats pass a law protecting the leprechauns on Slieve Foy. They refused. They said the existence of leprechauns could not be proved. I argued that as they are very rare and it's extremely difficult to prove their existence, the most anyone is going to get is a fleeting glimpse. Eventually they agreed to pass the law because they had to admit they could not prove that leprechauns don't exist!' So, thanks to Kevin's efforts Slieve Foy's leprechauns are included in the EU Habitats Directive, which protects the flora, fauna and leprechauns. If you don't believe me, look it up!

Leprechauns are fairy shoemakers. Like all fairies, they can grant wishes, but they are unwilling to do so because they are jealous of humans because humans have eternal life while they have to wait until Judgement Day to see if God gives it to them. Leprechauns are old and ugly, as are two other types of fairy, Cluricauns and Far Darrigs.

Cluricauns (Clobhair-ceann) spend their time getting drunk in rich men's cellars. You'll never see a sober Cluricaun! The Far Darrig (fear dearg translates as the Red Man because he always wears a red cap and coat) is nasty because he plays unpleasant, gruesome practical jokes. A typical example is to jump out from behind a tree and throw blood around somebody who is walking in a forest.

Another type of fairy, the Fear-Gorta (Man of Hunger), is very different. He's a phantom who looks like a bundle of skin and bones because he's been very hungry for a long time. He haunts the land during times of famine begging for help and he brings good luck to anyone who feeds him.

The Leanhaun Shee (fairy mistress – Shee means fairy) isn't small and ugly. She looks like a very beautiful woman. She'll never age, never die and she's pure evil. Her one aim is to seduce men. If she gets a man caught in her clutches she casts a spell from which escape is practically impossible. Her victim is unable to find peace and becomes thinner and thinner until eventually he dies. Even after death he won't find peace and will spend eternity as a miserable wandering ghost. The only possible escape is to get a friend interested in her so she switches allegiance. But there's one good thing about a Leanhaun Shee – she inspires her victims to write beautiful poetry.

Irish folklore says fairies tether their horses to ragwort (Jacobaea vulgaris), a very common and highly poisonous plant, that is usually regarded as a weed. It can grow as tall as 90cm (3ft). Frankly, I can't imagine tying a horse to it and find that piece of fairy lore hard to believe! Incidentally, in Scotland ragwort is also mythologically associated with Prince William (1721–60), the second son of King

Ragwort, where the fairies tether their horses.

George II, who accidentally sowed its seeds from food and bedding for his horses. It spreads very rapidly and became associated with him (he was also known as the Duke of Cumberland). He decimated staunch, presbyterian, rebel troops at the Battle of Culloden (1746). They called 'his' weed 'Stinking Billy', as it seemed to follow in his bloody footsteps wherever he went. At the same time a garden plant appeared, Dianthus barbatus, which was called 'Sweet William' by his supporters.

Fairies can turn nasty and steal humans, particularly good-looking ones. Some years ago I met a woman in Carlingford who told me she believed the fairies once intended to steal her brother. He'd taken his car to go to a dance in Dundalk. The whole family, apart from the brother, were at home in bed, fast asleep, when the mother woke up in a terrible state. She hauled everybody out of bed, much to their great annoyance, and made them go down to their farm kitchen, get down on their knees and pray. She said she knew the fairies were going to steal their brother and they needed to pray for his protection. They prayed until a short time after dawn, when they heard the brother's car chugging home. He was shivering with fear, crying and had his jacket on inside out. He said:

> I was coming home over the Cooley Mountains when I needed to pee. I stopped the car beside a gate of a field, went through it, did what I had to do then tried to come home. The trouble was I couldn't find the gate! It had disappeared. I walked all round the field, no gate! The atmosphere was, I can't describe it,

scary! I tried to calm down. I told myself I'd taken drink, so I was probably imagining things. Perhaps I hadn't gone round the whole field? I tied my handkerchief on a branch and stuck close to the hedge as I walked round the field again. I found my handkerchief, but no gate! By this time I was in a real panic. I started to think of all mother's daft notions and stories about fairies. Maybe she was right! Maybe fairies do steal people. I wished I'd listened more carefully. I remembered she said they don't steal ugly people, so I rubbed muck on my face and took my jacket off and turned it inside out to look ugly. I remembered her saying fairies don't like people to have food in their stomachs. Luckily I had a bar of chocolate in my pocket so I nibbled wee bits of it very slowly. The gate reappeared with the first light at dawn. It was near my handkerchief. I ran through it, got into my car and drove like the hammers and here I am!

The late John Campbell, a storyteller who lived in Mullaghabawn in County Armagh, told me one night he'd done a gig in Newcastle in County Down and was tired, so he decided to take a shortcut home by driving over the Mournes and through Mayo, rather than going round by the coast. He said, 'I knew I shouldn't have risked it! I knew there's a bridge near Mayo that belongs to the fairies and anyone who passes over it at night comes to harm. I got over it and had a bad puncture! Now that could have been a coincidence, but, it could have been the fairies!'

The number of stories like that are endless. As I said, I don't believe in fairies but I wouldn't risk annoying them!

GREAT FAMINE (1845–47)

During the nineteenth century there were many famines in Ireland. The worst one occurred between 1845 and 1847 and became known as the Great Famine. In actual fact it didn't end until 1851, because it took time for the country to recover. The population had grown rapidly during the seventeenth and eighteenth centuries. Land was at a premium and it was expensive. Rents were high. Standards of nutrition and housing were extremely poor. A large percentage of the population lived in houses that were built from sods and thatched with whatever happened to be available locally. Unfortunately, sod houses had a short life expectancy because they soaked up water in Ireland's damp climate. Desperate owners tried to prolong the life of their houses by propping them up with anything that was available, like branches of trees. The houses eventually became dangerous and collapsed on their unfortunate owners. People who were weak because of starvation, or suffering from cholera, or other diseases that were rife during the Great Famine, crawled into their sod houses and died. The house collapsed and buried them. This means that the number of deaths recorded, due to famine, is greatly underestimated. The census of 1842 shows that nearly half of the rural population in the north of Ireland lived in sod houses.

William Carleton, the nineteenth-century educationalist and writer, described sod houses as usually being windowless and recorded that green branches of willow were tied together to form a structure, called an old man of branches, or a corrag, 6ft in height (and much thicker than a sack). It was stood against the windy side of the door to provide shelter and its position was changed according to the direction of the wind. Furniture was a rarity. Most people slept on straw on damp floors and poverty was so grinding they were not clothed properly. They dressed in rags that did not cover their bodies modestly. Complete families, grandmother, father, mother, and perhaps five or six children, lived together in squalid conditions along with the family pig, which was referred to as 'the gentleman who pays the rent'. It was an important part of the rural economy as it sired piglets that could be sold. Pigs disappeared during the famine because families couldn't afford to feed them. On Friday, 22 January 1947, the *Belfast Newsletter* stated that every gentleman in the land should rear pigs and give them to the tenantry to be used as food. In the distant past pigs took the place of dogs, except you could eat a pig! Pigs were often educated so they were house trained and understood English, or Irish, or Ulster Scots, depending on the language spoken by the family. There's a story of a pig that understood English and Irish who wouldn't respond to a stranger speaking English if it had not been introduced by its owner!

Potatoes were the staple diet of the poor. They, with a drink of buttermilk, formed a reasonably balanced diet for the time, although there was a tendency for people living on it for about fifty years to become blind because it was lacking in Vitamin A. If the farmer could grow a few carrots the family was landed! The standard of living was so poor, living on a diet of potatoes wasn't thought to be a hardship. Famished people undercooked their potatoes because they stay in the stomach longer than soft ones as they are harder to digest.

Potatoes were introduced by Sir Walter Raleigh, probably around 1586. (He became Mayor of Youghall in 1588.) The poor usually had three meals a day, one at 8 a.m., one at 12 noon and one between 7 and 8 p.m. Potatoes were boiled in an iron pot and strained through a basket made of unpeeled willow. If the family was comparatively wealthy, the family sat on three-legged stools around a table and the potatoes were thrown on to it, usually with a cloth. If the family didn't have a table, the strainer containing the potatoes was set on top of the cooking pot and they were eaten directly from that. Many families didn't have plates or bowls, so they ate the potatoes with their hands. The family pig sat beside the youngest child and the pair often squabbled.

Potatoes left over from a meal were saved. Fishermen carried cold potatoes on their voyages, children took them to school for lunch, they were pushed into the embers of a fire to feed hungry strangers and they were fed to animals. Any potatoes that were left over were made into potato bread by being mixed with flour, a little milk, butter, rolled flat like dough and baked on a griddle. They were used to make rousel by mixing them with oatmeal and buttermilk, forming them into a rounded shape about 2in (5cm) deep and baking them on a griddle.

In the early 1800s before the Great Famine, the population expanded dramatically. As it grew, so did the pressure on land. Parents gave portions of their land to their children because they didn't want to see them starve. These children in their turn divided their land among their children, so in a comparatively short time there were many families settled on land that could only reasonably be expected to provide for one and farms became smaller and smaller. The Province of Ulster, which includes the six counties comprising Northern Ireland, had the greatest proportion of small farms in Ireland; that is, farms that were less than 5 acres. As the pressure on land increased, more and more unsuitable land was used. There are still traces of lazy beds, once used for the production of potatoes, in places such as on the top of Belfast's Cave Hill. Eventually the countryside became more densely populated than the towns. Competition for land caused rent increases, so those in Ireland were 80 to 100 per cent higher than in those in England.

The pressure on land became greater and greater as the population grew and the amount of human waste increased. It sank into the water table beneath the soil and seeped into wells, streams and rivers. There was no system of sewage disposal. Very wealthy people had flushing toilets. There was no satisfactory place to empty them, so the contents were stored in the basement and pumped out on to the streets at night. Storing the contents of flushing toilets in basements caused a stench on the ground floor and that was where the kitchen was located! Servants were expected not to mind awful smells! There was no appreciation of the necessity of hygiene, so houseflies weren't considered dangerous. They don't sting or bite, so why bother about them? Flies live and breed on manure. They also like sugar! They multiplied in sewage secreted in the basement, came into the kitchen and landed on food, spreading microscopic germs from manure and causing diseases from which people died. Young children were particularly vulnerable, especially babies. The fly population is at its maximum in September, which caused September weaning to be particularly dangerous and many more babies than usual died from infantile diarrhoea. Most wealthy people used chamber pots, also called 'goes-unders' (goes under the bed). As if all that wasn't enough, a further danger was described by the following letter printed on 23 December 1846 in a Fermanagh newspaper, the *Impartial Reporter*:

> Sir,
>
> I have just heard that it is intended to make a graveyard on the grounds of the poorhouse. Was there ever such a project? A place for burial in such a place!
>
> All under the poorhouse is limestone rock, through which water finds its way as rapidly as down a river course. Granted! Then bury hundreds of putrefied bodies, putrescence will flow into cisterns at the pumps, and what comforting reflections must occupy the minds of those who use the water, tea made out of stewed hag, and the master's whiskey punch diluted with essence of a boiled beggar man would be rare novelties.
>
> Disgusting,
Sir
Yours etc.,
An engineer

When Queen Victoria's husband, Prince Albert, died in December 1861 because he caught typhoid from contaminated water in Windsor Castle, the government began to take the importance of proper sewage disposal seriously and matters began to improve.

Shafto Adair was a landlord in the Ballymena area. (Local tradition states he was the subject of the song 'Bobby Shafto' and the Adair Arms Hotel in Ballymena is called after the family.) Ballymena is, and was, a thriving, prosperous town whose citizens have a reputation for hard work and thrift. It was the last place in Ireland where one would expect the effects of the famine to be felt, yet the description of what happened as told by Adair in a pamphlet published by James Ridgway of London in 1847) is horrendous. His pamphlet clearly shows that official statistics at the time were unreliable because the authorities did not know of the existence of thousands who died. It would appear that the statistics counted only those who were comparatively fortunate because their existence was recognised when they were helped by famine relief, or through the workhouse or through emigration.

If you crawled into a sod house, you died there with your family and had the house collapse on top of you, so officially speaking you were never born.

Adair described Ballymena as the largest linen-producing town in the north of Ireland, saying its inhabitants were prosperous and self-reliant. People who were comparatively well off, in that they weren't homeless, found they had to sell the family pig because they didn't have enough potatoes to feed themselves, never mind a pig. There were plenty of turnips, but pigs don't fatten on turnips. Bran was available, but smallholders couldn't afford it, so the only thing they could do was sell the grain when there wasn't even enough to feed them. As a result of all this misfortune they couldn't pay their rent and were in all probability evicted, so they joined the throngs of homeless.

Ballymena people were comparatively lucky because they had the option of working on linen looms and earning a little money. However, seed became so scarce and so expensive, tenant farmers couldn't afford it. The price for oat seed in Belfast on 3 February 1847 ranged from 58–64*s* for a hundredweight. In Glasgow similar seed was sold for 48*s* for a quarter of a ton, that is 5 hundredweights! (There are 20 hundredweights in a ton.) The Ballymena authorities decided to try and help by sending to Glasgow to buy seed to sell to local tenants. More and more people reached unbearable levels of starvation and went to the local workhouse. They scavenged for food and ate whatever they could find, including seaweed, nettles and charlock. Nettles and seaweed are basically good foods but charlock was terrible! It's a common weed with a yellow flower belonging to the cabbage family. It's edible and will sustain life, but it makes you sick.

Workhouses were harsh institutions. Families were separated and men and women were housed in different quarters. Husbands and wives couldn't see each other, or their children, who were also segregated according to sex. Inmates were forced to work hard doing useless tasks such as breaking stones. Food was in short supply and practically inedible. Workhouses became not only overcrowded, but chocked with inmates and people fought to get in. Terrible though the workhouse was, it was better than the alternative – starving to death on the streets outside. Many children became trapped in the workhouse. Their families were dead and there were no job opportunities for them outside. The authorities decided the best thing to do was to encourage them to, as Shafto Adair recorded, 'go forth to aid in cultivating and subduing those regions where willing industry will ensure remuneration'. Workhouse inmates 'weren't to look upon emigration as banishment, but as an opportunity to become prosperous' and, of course, ratepayers appreciated 'the benefits of relieving the labour market'.

The government of the time did try to help, but the problem was so large their attempts were unsuccessful. Before we judge their actions there are two questions we should ask ourselves: namely, how successful are we today in alleviating hunger in places like Ethiopia? And should we judge through the eyes of someone with the morals of the society at the time, rather than those of today? In the past people had very different beliefs. They were churchgoers with what we would consider a twisted view of Christianity. They sincerely believed that they should obey God's will. I'm not disagreeing with that but I do think their idea of God's will was very wrong. They believed that God causes suffering to punish people who have done wrong. The Irish were starving. They must, as a nation, have done something very sinful and were being chastised. It would be wrong to interfere with God's will. Today we have undergone a seismic change in that we believe we should try and help people who are unfortunate.

At first the government tried to arrange employment for the starving in the form of road works. That was not successful because it was so badly organised people died of starvation before they received their meagre wage. Famine roads were straight. Some of them were useless and have never been used. What use is a road that leads straight into a bog and stops? Others desecrated holy sites, or attempted to do so but were thwarted by the local population, as happened to the Holy Well on the outskirts of Belcoo (see Holy Wells). In 1847 outdoor relief was not permitted, so the authorities in Ballymena decided to organise a soup kitchen. The whole community came alive with a genuine desire to help the starving. Policemen, shopkeepers and soldiers contributed from their pay. A list was made of poor people living in the area and materials were bought to help them. The contributions of the Society of Friends (Quakers) towards famine relief was outstanding. They, like Shafto Adair, organised soup kitchens until the government took over that function.

Famine Stone on Antrim Coast Road.

Tenants were evicted if they could not pay their rent. (Cut out by Tinke Crowe and printed with her kind permission)

Great Famine Commemoration Stone, Lisnaskea.

Adair said the problem lay in the way in which land was leased. A lease was granted for a term of years, so a small piece of land, suitable for one family, could remain in that family for a very long time. The tenant sub-divided the land between his children, who in turn shared it with their children and so on. Adair tells of a case when the original lease expired there were 1,800 people found to be living on the land. There was a law passed after the Great Famine forbidding the division of land. It had to be willed to one person on the death of its owner. There's an old saying from the days of the workhouse:

Rattle my bones over the stones,
I'm a poor pauper who nobody owns.

Traces of the Great Famine remain in Northern Ireland to the present day in place names such as 'Hungry House Lane', at Magheragall, near Lisburn in County Antrim, and outside Armagh City on the road to Monaghan there is a house known locally as 'the porridge house' that tradition says marks the spot where people were fed porridge. Local historian Viki Herbert told me there is a place between Belturbet and Newtownbutler in County Fermanagh that is known as 'Starvation Row'.

FINTONA RAILWAY

In the 1830s in Fintona, a small town in County Tyrone, it was decided a railway link between the town and the main railway line would be useful to transport wood. A committee was set up and spent considerable time debating the form the future railway should take. It must be remembered that this was in the very early days of railways, which were a new form of transport. Many things we take for granted had to be discussed in considerable detail. One of the first decisions concerned the advisability of laying rail tracks. They decided it was much easier to pull heavy loads along rails than over rough tracks, so yes! Rail tracks were necessary!

The next big decision was what sort of power should be used to pull the train? Stephenson's steam engine had been invented but most of the committee members were against such new-fangled developments. They felt a steam engine could be very dangerous. It might explode and at best be unreliable, so they decided it would be wiser to stick to horse power. Obviously their horse would have to be a large powerful beast, so the decision was made to buy a Clydesdale.

In Victorian society one knew one's place and one stayed in it! Poor people were not allowed to mix with rich ones. Perish the thought! The committee wondered how the classes were to be separated and decency should be maintained on the train? They decided poor people should travel on the roof and the wealthy charged a premium for sitting inside. The inside compartment was divided into two compartments, one for first-class passengers and the other for the second class. The coach man sat on the roof along with the third-class customers. That was very dangerous because horses are unpredictable. The roof was overcrowded. People, including the coach man, could fall off! There were several accidents and some of them were fatal. The passengers sitting on the roof gave the early carriages the appearance of a stagecoach rather than anything to do with a railway. The committee bought a horse, christened it Dick, and established a tradition. All their horses were called Dick. It didn't matter what sort of a horse it was, its name was Dick.

The Londonderry and Enniskillen Railway opened a branch line to Fintona on 5 June 1853. It proved very successful. It was not the fastest railway on earth, so passengers had ample time to admire the scenery as Dick ambled along. My old friend, the late Tom McDevitte, also known as Barney McCool, said, 'Once, when I was sitting ensconced comfortably inside a carriage, I was filled with joy when I saw a butterfly fly past the train. It was comparatively speeding!'

The successive 'Dicks' were stabled overnight in a long shed. The last Dick was a gelding, looked after by the last driver, Willie McClean. He treated Dick like a member of his own family. Dick recognised Willie's footsteps and whinnied whenever he heard them. By this time the design of the railway had been influenced by the appearance of horse-drawn trams, which were introduced into Belfast in 1872, and Willie's 'train' looked more like a tram than a stage coach. Willie could stay inside rather than perch perilously on the roof. He worked on the line until it closed in 1957. The strict class system had been dropped and passengers could sit wherever they liked. Once this caused problems. The usual passengers took their usual seats when a crowd of strangers arrived. They were odoriferous! The regular passengers complained. Willie dealt with the situation with his usual tact. He announced, 'Will all the passengers at the back-end tram please get off and sit at the front because the back end isn't going!' That worked. The strangers travelled first class and the normal passengers second.

Jack Griffins, a young lad, came to work as a porter around 1947. One morning Dick was lying on the ground. Willie told Jack that Dick was very ill and asked for help to get the horse on its feet. Dick walked unsteadily to his stable and lay down again. That was a bad sign. Willie said, 'I think Dick's in pain. He keeps looking down his side. He could be suffering from indigestion.' He got a pound of Epsom salts, mixed it with water and asked Jack to help pour it down Dick's throat. It had no effect whatsoever, so they sent for Ernie Johnston, the local vet. Ernie got a foul, thick black substance, mixed it in a basin, and the three of them managed to pour it down Dick's throat. 'There!' said Ernie. 'That should fix him.' 'On top of what I've given him?' asked Willie. When the vet heard about the Epsom salts he said, 'I'm sorry lads. Poor Dick's had it! The only thing you can do is lock him in his stable and close the door.'

After the vet had left Willie said, 'Here Jack, give us a hand. I'll no close no door on poor old Dick. Let's get him up and ring him.' They got Dick up, took him into the yard and walked him round in circles. The poor horse didn't want to move, so Jack gave him encouragement by walking behind with a whip. After a while Dick's sides began to heave. Willie shouted, 'Stand back Jack!' Jack got out of the way as Dick let fly, producing enough dung to fill a wheelbarrow. It was said the stench stretched down line from Fintona to Dromore. Dick was cured! He ate a hearty meal and was back at work the next day. Willie said, 'I think the trouble was caused by a feed of fresh hay!'

FERMANAGH GEOPARK AND MARBLE ARCH CAVES

A geopark is a region of scientific importance encompassing geological heritage along with educational purposes, local communities and folklore. It must be capable of development that is sustainable.

Fermanagh's geopark stretches from County Fermanagh, which is part of Northern Ireland in the United Kingdom of Great Britain and Northern Ireland, which has a devolved government situated in Belfast in Stormont, responsible to Westminster, into County Cavan, part of the south of Ireland, which is a different state, ruled from Dublin. The landscape it encompasses is stunning. It contains many places of archaeological and historical interest, including Iron Age forts, prehistoric tombs and early Christian monasteries as well as Marble Arch Caves, Big Dog Forest, Carrigan Forest, Moneygashel Cashel and Gortmaconnell Viewpoint.

I spent a happy morning with Richard Watson in Marble Arch Caves before he retired. He told me he applied for the job of caves warden in 1985 because he wanted to work 'somewhere out of the ordinary'. During the time he worked there 18,000 hectares of West Fermanagh became designated as a global geopark.

He helped shape the caves and the visitor centre facility. They are now one of Fermanagh's most successful tourism products and he's proud of what has been achieved. He said:

> I might have been the front of house person, but it was a big collective effort. There was a great team behind me, including staff from the Marble Arch Caves Geopark, Fermanagh and Omagh District Council and the various partner organisations we have worked with over the years. The opportunity to get in there at the beginning was an added bonus because you could put your own stamp on it.

He began by spending time helping prepare the finishing touches to the lofty chambers of the show caves, the natural underworld of rivers, the winding passages, the content of the tour and other operational procedures such as health and safety, most of which remain consistent today. He was surprised and delighted as the caves were an instant success and hit their projected three-year visitor number figure within the first week of opening! Since then the visitor centre has undergone three major expansions, in 1989, 1998 and 2014.

Marble Arch Caves. (Printed with kind permission of Marble Arch Caves)

Richard told me in the past people living on Cuilcagh Mountain used to use the Marble Arch, from which the caves get their name, over the upper end of upstream Cladagh Glen, as a road. One day a young girl called Maggie Duffy was running over the bridge when she tripped and fell into the river below. Fortunately she was wearing very wide skirts and they opened like a parachute and deposited her gently in the water, where she was rescued. He also told me to ignore any stories about elephants living in the caves. They are tall tales that originated in a local bar. What happened was in 1912 a group of German tourists were walking along beside the River Cladagh when they saw elephants drinking its waters. They were very surprised. They didn't think elephants lived in Ireland, so they went to the nearest pub and asked the bartender. He said, with a perfectly straight face:

> There was once a local landlord who was very wealthy and who loved to travel. He went to India and brought elephants to Ireland. Sometime later he sold his estate here and went to live in England, leaving his elephants behind. They appear very happy. They eat the local vegetation, drink the river water and when the weather turns cold, they shelter in Marble Arch Caves.

What he didn't tell the tourists was that Duffy's Circus had elephants and they were visiting Fermanagh at the time.

G

GHOSTS

Northern Ireland is full of ghosts and stories about them are enough to fill several books. Some places have multiple ghosts, so I'm going to choose a couple of my favourites. They are associated with places it is possible to visit. Lissan House is said to be the most haunted house in the whole of Northern Ireland. It has a very interesting history, as well as memorable ghosts, so I'm giving it a place to itself.

The Hillsborough Ghost

Hillsborough Castle is now owned by the Crown Estates. It's more of a large family home than a castle. Both the house and gardens are open to the public and are well worth visiting.

The castle was originally owned by the Marquis of Downshire, whose family name was Hill. Hillsborough gets its name after the Hills, who left Northern Ireland at the Partition of Ireland in 1921. After that the castle housed Lord Gray, the then Lieutenant of Northern Ireland. Lady Gray was an aunt of the late Queen Elizabeth II, so she and her sister Princess Margaret spent a lot of their childhood there. They grew to love the castle and grounds, and I'm sure they heard the love story and song associated with it.

Lord Arthur Hill (1846–1931), a younger son of the Marquess of Downshire, was a sad, lonely widower when his sisters invited their friend, Annie Fortesque Harrison (1848–1944), to stay with them in the castle. Annie was a beautiful, talented girl. She loved music, enjoyed playing the piano, the organ and composing songs. The young couple were soulmates and fell deeply in love.

There was a rigid class system in vogue at the time. One did not marry outside one's station! Annie was a lovely person, but she was not in the same social league as Lord Arthur and the Hill family traditionally married for money.

One evening Annie overheard someone saying:

> Anyone can see Annie Harrison and Lord Hill are greatly attracted to her each other. She should realise she is not of a suitable station in society to make a suitable wife for the likes of him. If she really cared for him, and I believe she does, she should leave the castle and enable Lord Arthur to find someone suitable to marry. At the moment she's spoiling his chances.

Poor Annie was heartbroken but thought the gossips were right. She knew Lord Arthur loved her. He would not look at another woman while she was around, so the best thing she could do was slip away silently without giving him the chance to argue with her and make her change her mind so she wrote a polite 'Thank you' letter and left quietly.

Lord Hill was heartbroken. He attempted to find her and failed. She had not left a forwarding address.

Two years later one of Annie's music compositions, 'In the Gloaming', was published and became a hit, top of the then pops!

> In the gloaming, oh, my darling! when the lights are dim and low,
> And the quiet shadows, falling, softly come and softly go,
> When the winds are sobbing faintly with a gentle, unknown woe,
> Will you think of me and love me, As you did once, long ago?
>
> In the gloaming, oh, my darling! think not bitterly of me!
> Tho' I pass'd a way in silence, left you lonely, set you free,
> For my heart was crush'd with longing; what had been could never be.
> It was best to leave you thus, dear,
> Best for you, and best for me,
>
> Music by Annie Fortescue Harrison, Lyrics by Meta Orred

Lord Hill recognised the tune and the sentiment. He managed to trace Annie through her publisher, flew to her side and told her if she wouldn't marry him he would remain lonely and single. He wasn't going to look for a 'suitable match'. He brought her back to Hillsborough Castle. They got married and were very happy.

Lord Arthur Hill gave Annie an organ, which is now in Hillsborough Parish Church at the bottom of the hill. Annie erected a memorial to Lord Arthur and his first wife. It's in the nave to the left of the church when facing the altar. This is the church royalty attend when they are resident in the castle – it has several interesting artefacts associated with them, such as signatures.

'Annie Harrison is not a suitable match for Lord Arthur!'

It is said that the ghosts of Lord Arthur Hill and Annie Fortescue Harrison haunt Hillsborough. People say they have heard the sound of hooves coming up the street leading to the castle, and when they look out their windows they see a coach and four coming up hill. It stops at the door of the castle and a handsome young man helps a beautiful young lady to alight. They look so happy it would make your glass eye water!

I have a friend, Nigel McKelevy, who has an apartment in one of the Georgian buildings adjacent to the castle. He says he has heard the sounds of a coach pulled by horses. He looked out of the window but there was nothing there.

The Ghost in Killeavy Old Church Graveyard

The ghost that haunts the grounds of Killeavy Old Church in South Armagh is very different. It's not gentle and loving, but malicious and harmful. It nearly claimed the life of a young girl, called Anne, who lived with her granny, near the gates of Killeavy Old Church. Every Saturday night she used to walk, alone, to the céili house behind the graveyard for a bit of craic. She was very attractive, so young men pleaded to see her safely home. When the céili was over she refused all offers, walked over to the graveyard's wall and used spaces in the worn brickwork to climb over the top and take a shortcut through the graveyard. The more Anne played hard to get, the keener the boys were to catch her. One night, two of the boys thought they'd frighten her by dressing up as a ghost. Anne heard giggling and guessed they were planning some sort of mischief.

'I bet,' she thought, ' those big fools are going to pretend they're ghosts. I don't believe in ghosts. I'll go home by a different path and they can freeze to death waiting to scare me.'

Killeavy Old Church.

She sauntered slowly over to the graveyard wall, climbed on to the top, jumped down and wended her way along a path she'd never walked before. Suddenly a large figure leapt from behind a tomb stone. Anne nearly jumped out of her skin, then laughed, 'That was a good trick. You made me jump. I don't believe in ghosts. You don't scare me.' And with that she pulled the sheet away and ran laughing towards her home.

Her friends were sitting around the fire with Granny. Anne told them how the boys had tried to frighten her, showed them the sheet and threw it into the corner. About an hour later, two very cold boys entered. One of them said, 'Thon was a dead loss! We didn't see a soul.'

'Nonsense,' snapped Anne. 'I pulled a sheet off you.'

'No you didn't! You mustn't have gone your usual way home.'

Anne said, 'Yes, I guessed you were up to something. Quit codding. I pulled the sheet off you.'

'No you didn't, we have our sheet here,' and they held it up.

Granny went very white. 'I think we should have a look at those sheets,' she said.

They examined the sheets in the firelight and saw the boys' one was clean and had folds left from when it had been ironed. Anne's sheet was stained and slimy and bore a faint stench of decay.

'Ooh!' she yelled. 'That's horrible! Should I throw it on the fire?'

'No,' said one of the girls, 'I think if you steal something that belongs to the dead you have to give it back, or be cursed. Don't do anything until we get advice.'

'But I didn't steal anything,' sobbed Anne.

'Anne, we know you wouldn't steal anything but you took that shroud. You must give it back to its owner.'

'How do I give it back?'

'I don't know. We should ask the priest. He knows all about ghosts.'

'Anne,' said one of the boys, 'you should go immediately. This is an emergency. We don't know how long you've got before the curse works, or even if you are cursed.'

'But,' said Anne, 'it's an imposition. I'm a Presbyterian, not a Catholic.'

'That doesn't matter. Your minister's a fine man, but he's not into ghosts, while the parish priest knows all about them. Come on! We'll go with you.'

They set off down the road to the priest's house and told him the whole story. He was very upset. He said, 'You're right. Anne's in great danger. We've got to get that shroud back to its owner. I suggest you hang it on the hedge nearest the graveyard. The ghost may reclaim it and the danger'll be over. If it's still there in the morning, come back to me and I'll tell you what to do next. But let's pray that's not necessary.'

'What happens if somebody steals it?' Anne asked nervously.

'That's their problem, not yours. The curse will leave you and fall on them.'

The young people did what the priest suggested and went home to bed.

Poor Anne lay awake all night, praying and shivering with fear. At first light she went to the window and peered out. The shroud was still hanging on the hedge. She dressed quickly and ran to the priest's house. He saw her coming, opened the door and said, 'I take it from the look on your face the shroud's still there.'

Anne burst into tears. He put his arm around her shoulders and drew her gently into his house as he said, 'This is going to be difficult and very frightening. You must find a newborn baby and take it into the graveyard about ten o'clock at night. The evil spirit can't touch an innocent child, so you'll be safe. Wrap yourself and the baby up warmly, then keep it tight against your body. Hold the shroud out with your other hand so it can be clearly seen. The ghost will have to reclaim it and you will be free. Go alone. The ghost will kill anyone with you.'

Anne spent a miserable day attempting to 'borrow' a baby. Nobody would lend her one. Parents were unwilling to allow their babies go into the graveyard at night. Nine o'clock at night found Anne and Granny crying beside the fire when the door opened and in came the Presbyterian clergyman with his wife and baby daughter. 'Anne dear,' he said, 'we're so sorry to have been so thoughtless and to have allowed you to be so frightened. We were hoping somebody would lend you a baby but that hasn't happened so you can take our daughter.'

'Do you mean it?' Anne gasped through her tears.

'Yes dear,' the wife replied. 'We mean it. We'll stay here with Granny and pray for you until you get back.'

Just before ten o'clock Anne dressed warmly, wrapped the baby in a woollen rug and headed towards the churchyard. She shuddered as she lifted the shroud off the hedge and entered. The baby seemed unconcerned. It gurgled, cuddled close to Anne, then closed its eyes and fell asleep. Anne walked up and down the graveyard. Up and down, up and down through the dark, menacing, evil space, shivering with fear. Eleven o'clock struck, twelve o'clock, one o'clock, two o'clock, three o'clock, four o'clock. Her heart was in despair.

'This isn't working,' she thought, 'I'm doomed. Doomed!'

Tears ran down her face when suddenly a ghastly figure jumped out from behind a headstone.

Anne screamed.

The baby woke and yelled lustily.

The figure grabbed the shroud and put it on.

A decayed finger with green flesh hanging off it appeared around the edge of the shroud and pointed at Anne. An evil voice cackled, 'If it weren't for that innocent child, I'd kill you!' and disappeared.

Anne sobbed with relief and fear as she stumbled to the gate where Granny, the cleric and his wife were huddled together. 'We heard you scream and came to see what we could do,' Granny explained as they helped Anne back into the house.

The next Saturday night when one of the fellas asked Anne if he could see her home, she said 'Yes!'

She married him, lived happily and had nineteen children.

Local people say the ghost came back many years later when a young couple were making love in the graveyard. The man opened his eyes and saw something that scared him so much he had a heart attack and died. She was so traumatised she committed suicide three weeks later.

I'll tell you something, nothing would make me go into Killeavy Old Church after dark. I wouldn't risk it. I found walking around the old graveyard during daylight a creepy experience. I was glad to leave it! If you want to visit the graveyard, travel along the A1 motorway around Newry and follow the B113. The churchyard is signposted and it's approximately 3 miles from Newry. It's very different from Killeavy Castle, which is situated along the same narrow road.

Killeavy Castle.

Killeavy Castle feels haunted, but in a nice way by loving spirits who give the property a sense of peace and beauty. It was originally an old farmhouse that was bought by the Foxall Family in the 1830s. Meredith Foxall was a founder of a bank in Newry called Moore, McCann and Foxall. The bank crashed in 1816, but the Foxall family managed to salvage enough money to enable Powell Foxall to commission extensive repairs and additions to Killeavy Lodge in 1836. He and his predecessor, Joseph Foxall, were responsible for the beautiful woodlands that cover a considerable part of Slieve Gullion.

The present owners, Mike Boyle and his wife Pauline, grew up in the neighbourhood, and spent twenty-five years in Australia before coming home to South Armagh. They found the old Killeavy estate was in a dilapidated state, but the gentle spiritual atmosphere enchanted them, so they bought it. Inspired by the environment, they restored the old castle and built a new hotel that looks extremely modern but which incorporates the old farmhouse and stable block. Everything has a purpose. A lot of thought has gone into combating climate change and developing a sustainable business. At present they are restocking their woodland with native oak trees to restore habitat diversity. They are also developing forest trails to bring clients close to nature. There's a farm shop and a walled garden. It's all well worth a visit.

H

HANS SLOANE AND THE BRITISH MUSEUM

Sir Hans Sloane (1660–1753), one of the best-known figures in eighteenth-century England, was born in Killyleagh, County Down, and died in London. He was a fashionable physician, naturalist, collector and philanthropist. His collections formed the basis of the British Museum.

It is thought that Sir Hans' early education was in Killyleagh. He wrote, in the first volume of his book *A Voyage to the Islands Madera, Barbados Nieves, Saint Christophers and Jamaica* (1707), 'I had from my youth up been much pleased with the study of plants and other parts of nature.' Killyleagh would have been a wonderful place to encourage that interest. It is surrounded by lush countryside, and there is an abundance of wildfowl and varieties of seaweed. Killyleagh is very proud of its famous son and has erected a fine statue to him near the shore.

When Hans was 16, he became very ill and spent considerable time confined to his bedroom. However, three years later he was so much better he was able to travel to London to study medicine. He lodged in the Apothecaries' Hall in Blackfriars, where he 'acquired a perfect knowledge of the preparation and uses of most chemical medicines'. He also studied anatomy, physics and botany.

Hans studied for a year in London, then travelled to Paris to attend lectures in the Hôpital de la Charité before going south to study at the University of Orange. He couldn't be awarded a degree in Paris because he was a Protestant, but the University of Orange was a liberal institution that had been founded by William, Prince of Orange, afterwards William III of England. He was awarded his degree before studying at Montpellier, which was then one of the most outstanding medical schools in Europe.

Shortly after Hans returned to London, he was appointed physician to the Duke of Albemarle, who had been appointed Governor of Jamaica. Hans accompanied him to Jamaica. He stayed there for twenty months, increased his knowledge of medicine and botany, and was inspired to write *A Voyage to the Islands Madera, Barbados, Nieves, Saint Christophers and Jamaica* (2 vols, 1707–25). It was here that he started collecting plants and curiosities.

When the Duke of Albemarle died, his widow appointed him as her personal physician. They returned to London, where she introduced him to fashionable practice. He married a rich widow, Elizabeth Langley, whose husband had been a sugar planter. They set up house in Russell Street in Bloomsbury and had four children, of whom only two girls survived.

HELLFIRE CLUBS

In the eighteenth century, bored high-society rakes established exclusive clubs where members worshipped the Devil and held Black Masses, lit by black candles with crucifixes hung upside down. Members of Hellfire Clubs, also known as the Order of the Friars, of St Francis of Wycombe, had a ferocious black cat for a mascot and at their meetings they always left an empty chair for the Devil. These Devil-worshipping clubs appear to have existed for quite some time, and there are many hair-raising tales about them.

My favourite Hellfire story concerns Squire Hawkins. He'd been an alderman for King Charles II's army and it was his responsibility to feed and clothe the soldiers. As he'd done a good job, the king gave him lands around Rathfriland.

Squire Hawkins was a member of the Hellfire Club. He lived in Rathfriland's square with his good-living Christian wife, who attended Drumballyroney Church, which was about 2 miles from their home. He was a mean, cruel landlord. He, along with his Hellfire shenanigans, was hated and feared by the good people of Rathfriland and his God-fearing wife. He literally gave her hell! During his last illness he repeatedly told her he did not want a Christian burial. No way! He was a Devil worshipper and intended to stay that way. She decided otherwise and arranged for his body to be buried in Drumballyroney churchyard. It took eight horses fifteen hours to drag the carriage carrying his body to the churchyard because it was so reluctant to go. When the horses reached the gate of the graveyard they reared up and refused to enter, so the body had to be manhandled to its final resting place to be interred. The next Sunday, when the rector was giving his sermon, a bolt of lightning thundered down on Squire Hawkins' grave and split the horizontal tombstone to form the sign of the cross. When the rector looked out of the window he saw the Devil peering out of the grave! It gave him, and the congregation, a nasty scare! You can visit Squire Hawkins' grave. Go to Banbridge and follow the road leading to Rathfriland. The graveyard is signposted. Walk past the church door, round the side of the building and you'll find a dip in the earth. At the bottom of that dip there's a horizontal tombstone with a distinct split in the shape of a cross.

Squire Hawkins' grave.

The late Frank O'Dowd took me to see a house on the right-hand side of the road when travelling from Gilford to Lurgan. It was a beautiful place with a lovely conservatory at the side. 'That's gorgeous!' I breathed. Frank didn't say anything. We parked the car at the entrance and walked up the driveway. As we drew closer and closer to the house I felt more and more uneasy. There was something about the place that made a shiver shimmy up my spine. 'Well?' asked Frank. I looked him straight in the eye and said, 'I've a terrible feeling I want to get out of here!' Frank laughed and said, 'That makes two of us! This place looks beautiful but it feels evil. Come on back to the car and I'll tell you its story.'

Frank told me a previous owner of the house had been a dedicated member of the Hellfire Club. He was such a nasty man his wife left him, taking their children with her, and one by one all the servants left, leaving him with one faithful manservant. Eventually the owner became ill and died. His manservant was by the bedside with his boss at the time. The poor man was terribly upset because when his master breathed his last breath a black dog jumped out of the bed, down the stairs and out the door! There was a curse on the house that affected subsequent owners, who suffered terribly. They either died, or their families died, or they went bankrupt. Eventually the house got such a bad reputation it became impossible to sell it. Since then it's been knocked down and a housing estate has been built on the site.

Another story tells of a member of the Hellfire Club who was standing in front of a roaring fire drinking salthpeen (hot whiskey and melted butter) when the marrow in his bones melted and he fell to the floor.

Members of Hellfire Clubs always left an empty chair for the Devil. Once their mascot, a ferocious black cat, was present when a brave clergyman attended one of their meetings. He started to shiver, became petrified with fear and yelled,

'That's not a cat! That's the Devil.' The club members were so annoyed they decided to kill him. He asked for a few moments to pray before he was murdered. His wish was granted and during his prayers he exorcised the cat, which changed into the Devil and shot up the chimney and the clergyman escaped!

HIGHWAYMEN

Highwaymen were once a hazard for travellers. Taxes and rents were high and the highwaymen were usually popular because they robbed the rich and gave to the poor. Half-Hung McNaughton was an exception. He kept anything he stole. He came from a rich family and had a good job working for the government as a tax collector. Unfortunately he loved to gamble, lost all his own money and started losing money belonging to the government. To escape justice he 'disappeared' and became a highwayman.

McNaughton's good friend, Andrew Knox, lived in a large house at Prehen, which is now part of Derry/Londonderry. He had a very beautiful 15-year-old daughter called Mary Ann, who fell deeply in love with McNaughton. Her father was incensed. He believed McNaughton was wooing Mary Ann because he wanted to get access to her fortune and use it to pay off his debts, and at 39 years of age he was far too old for his daughter. He forbade the young couple to meet. In the time-honoured method of thwarted lovers, they kept in contact by writing letters to each other and leaving them hidden in a crevice in a tree. Mary Ann's father planned to take her away in the hope that she would forget McNaughton. The couple swore undying love and arranged for McNaughton to dress in his highwayman gear and kidnap her. He did as they planned and stopped the coach in which she was travelling with her father. There was a fracas in which McNaughton accidentally shot and killed Mary Ann and wounded her father. He escaped but was eventually captured and locked up in Lifford jail. He was tried and sentenced to death 'by hanging on the great road between Lifford and Strabane'. He climbed up on the gallows, the hangman put the rope around his neck and attempted to drop him to his death. The rope broke and McNaughton fell on the ground unhurt. Anyone who survived hanging was granted a full pardon, but McNaughton got up, climbed back on the gallows and shouted, 'I don't want to be known as Half-Hung McNaughton. I don't want to live without Mary Ann. I don't want to be pardoned! I demand to be hung!' He put the rope around his neck and jumped off the gallows so forcibly that he died instantly because his neck was broken in the fall.

Some years ago I had an interesting discussion with an acquaintance in Derry/Londonderry. We laughed heartily at the so-called ghost that haunted a roundabout outside Toomebridge. It had a scary white face, was dressed in white floating material, appeared at dusk, and ran along beside traffic occasionally waving through the window at lone occupants in cars before disappearing. The 'ghost' became locally famous. People started going out looking for it. Ghost hunters need sustenance supplied by local hotels, restaurants and pubs, so the town's business improved and the roundabout became a traffic hazard. The 'ghost' was eventually caught by the police, found to be what locals call a 'big lig' (joker), arrested, tried in court and let off with a caution.

I remembered Half-Hung McNaughton is reputed to haunt the road on which he was hung. I asked my acquaintance if that ghost ever appeared? 'Oh yes!' he replied. 'The ghost is now in Altnagelvan Hospital. He's suffering from concussion with fourteen stitches in his head.' He went on to explain that the 'ghost' was his brother-in-law, who thought that a 'presence' near Strabane would improve business in the town, as it had done for Toomebridge. He dressed up in suitable gear and set out one Saturday to haunt the road between Strabane and Derry/Londonderry. Unfortunately he chose the night of what was a rare event – Strabane's team won a Gaelic football match against what they considered to be their rivals, Derry/Londonderry. There was great jubilation and great were the celebrations of the winners and their supporters. They filled a double-decker bus and had enjoyed becoming the worse for wear in a pub before setting off for home. When they saw the ghost they decided there were more spirits inside them than outside, got off the bus and stoned it. That particular ghostly highwayman was well and truly laid!

Redmond O'Hanlon was a very different kind of highwayman. He was very popular with the locals because he was a kind of Robin Hood. He really did rob the rich and give to the poor. Many Irish men, Protestant and Catholic clergymen as well as many members of the militia, supported him and gave him information, as did members of the public. He convinced many landlords they wanted to pay protection money. It was said his protection was so good you didn't even have to bar your doors at night if you were in his care. Eventually he had an income that was larger than that of the king's revenue men. The authorities grew to hate him and in 1674 put a price on his head. He was wanted dead or alive. He became neurotic about his safety and hired bodyguards. That was a mistake because one night, while he slept near Hilltown, one of his guards, namely his stepbrother, Art McCall O'Hanlon, murdered him, received the reward and was pardoned.

'Redmond O'Hanlon? Haven't heard of him, haven't seen him and don't speak of him.'

Thanks to the actions of highwaymen, and others with evil intentions, the old roads kept to high ground where possible because it was easier to spot highwaymen approaching. In places it's possible to trace parts of ancient roads beside modern highways. The old roads were narrow dirt tracks. Sometimes their existence is marked by place names, such as 'Old Coach Road'.

Local residents can often tell of the existence of an old road from oral history handed down through the centuries. When I moved into my present residence, in Banbridge, I was told the road on which I had gone to live was part of the old coach road leading from the north to the south of Ireland! It runs up hill and down dale parallel to the present A1 motorway. By simply following the road and asking residents, I was able to trace it to the point where it crossed the A1. In other places it's not as easy to trace as it deviates from the A1, goes along a track and has been obliterated, becoming what is now part of a field. The route can be picked up from old maps and in places it's possible to imagine the time it was haunted by highwaymen.

Maintenance of the old roads was by way of toll houses. Unfortunately only one survives. It has been thoughtfully incorporated in a private residence on the motorway near Dromore.

HOLY WELLS

The patron saint of Ireland, St Patrick, didn't bring Christianity to Ireland. There were several missionaries before him. What he did do was make Christianity widespread and popular. He spent his time as a slave on Slemish Mountain, in County Antrim, then when he returned to Ireland he landed on Strangford Lough, in County Down. His first church was founded at Saul, again in County Down, and he founded a cathedral in Armagh, which pre-dates Canterbury Cathedral and is recognised as the ecclesiastical centre of the whole of Ireland. He is buried in the grounds of Downpatrick Cathedral. He also founded a number of holy wells throughout Ireland, many of them being in Northern Ireland.

Holy wells are credited with having healing powers. One of the traditions when visiting such a well is to leave some sort of token behind, so there is often a tree or a fence to which scraps of cloth have been tied. The idea is if you're hoping to be given something by the well, it's only polite to give something back! There are so many wells that space does not permit them all to be mentioned, so I'm going to pick out a couple of my favourites.

St Patrick's Well at Belcoo

I found it difficult to find Belcoo, never mind find its holy well, named after St Patrick, who it is said gave it the ability to cure disease. The reason for my difficulty is that the roads in County Fermanagh weave in and out over the border into the south of Ireland. Southerners frequently do not signpost places on the other side of the border. I started my journey to Belcoo from Florencecourt. I followed a signpost and Belcoo appeared to disappear. All I could find was a settlement called Blacklion. Eventually I gave up, turned into Blacklion to ask for directions, crossed a bridge and discovered I was in Belcoo! It's the other part of the settlement, which is cut in two by the border!

One half of the village is curious. There's a signpost in the middle pointing to the holy well, which is close by. It is beautiful with a lovely peaceful atmosphere and larger than I expected.

I met Mairéad O'Dolan, author of *Church Ruins Stone Monuments Near the Holy Well Belcoo*. Her family are its traditional keepers. She said, 'I have heard it said that the water is cold in summer and warm in winter. I have experienced wading in both seasons and know this to be true.' She disagreed with what Isaac Butler said in 1740 when he described it as 'the best cold bath in the Kingdom, a spring exceedingly transparent and cold'. It is possible to swim in it.

The Holy Well at Belcoo.

The Ordnance Survey Memoirs of Ireland for 1835 states, 'the tradition of the olden times is that St Patrick sojourned in the parish for some time and that the holy well was an object of his peculiar favour as he endowed it with many miraculous privileges'.

People used to walk long distances to visit the well to collect some water hoping it would cure a loved one. The well's water has been credited with curing stomach problems, depression, warts and eczema, among other complaints.

In 1739 Dean Henry, the Rector of Killesher, described the way in which people bathed in the holy well as indecent. He referred to drunkenness and debauchery, which caused the clergy to attempt to stop the pilgrimage. They didn't succeed, as recorded in the O.S. Memoirs of 1834:

> Some of the old inhabitants remember when the well was enclosed by a wall and had a small gate which was kept constantly locked and individuals who wanted to use the water were obliged to pay a small sum to the person who kept it. Doulagh Donagh (sic), or the last Sunday in July each year, was the station day and crowds of diseased persons from every part of the country attended; and that the blind have received their sight and the lame thrown away their crutches at the well is attested by individuals residing in the neighbourhood.

Maíréad O'Dolan told me the holy well is still used to cure people. She was once phoned by a woman who asked to be taken to the well because her son had committed suicide and she couldn't sleep. Even though it was outside the pilgrimage time, Maíréad, the woman and her daughter made the stations. About a week later the woman phoned to say she could sleep again.

The correct way to do the stations is described on a leaflet in *The Pilgrim's Manual*, which may be found in the box attached to the fence. Or you can get it from the Leonard family. They live in the bungalow opposite the gate. It takes about an hour to make them.

In 1957, Father Leyden, the curate at the time, asked older people to record the prayers and the traditional way of doing the stations.

In April 2000, Father Ó Ríordáin thought it would be a good thing if people from all denominations could come and do the stations. He was asked to write alternative prayers for that purpose. As a result the *Pilgrim's Manual* contains the traditional way (TW) and the alternative way (AW).

Every year a weekly pilgrimage to the well runs from the last Sunday in July until 15 August. It is advertised locally and people are available to lead the pilgrims. In the past the pilgrimage was done in groups of twos and threes and that's still considered the best way.The busy main road between Belcoo and Garrison is a hazard as it cuts across the path of the pilgrimage. There are traffic warning signs in place and pilgrims are warned of the danger. Strong sticks are provided to help balance in and around the mill stream.

On many occasions the holy well has been in danger of extinction. One of the most serious threats was caused by the government during the years of the Great Famine. The government organised road works to provide work for the starving. Roderick Grey was the county surveyor for Fermanagh at the time. Famine roads are straight and he was a fanatic regarding keeping rules. He designed a road that cut straight through the middle of the holy well's site with a bridge over it, and would not change his mind. As far as he was concerned, his road had to go over the well.

Local people were very annoyed and used the cover of night for 'wee fairies' to undo the previous day's work and restore the well. Eventually, Roderick Grey realised the road would never be finished if he didn't adjust his plans and the well was saved. The road goes round it!

A fair used to be held locally during the time of pilgrimage. Malachy O'Dolan told Maíráid that twenty-three shebeens (also called síbíns, illegal drinking dens) were at the fair. James Rogers wrote in The *Impartial Reporter* in 1926:

Whiskey was cheap in those far off days as duty was low and the best of it, a native product, paid none at all; the licensed trade (to use the modern term) was fully represented in the form of numerous tents erected in the fair green, well stocked with liquor, warranted not to contain more than one headache a gallon.

There was a class now almost extinct without which no fair years ago was regarded as complete. I refer to the travelling tinkers. Although no great respecters of laws, moral, religious or civil, the tinker appealed to the Irish character largely because there was in the class something of the element of the picturesque and a great deal of the rollicking devil-may-care.

There was generally a little bloodletting before the fair was over; that goes without saying, for no fair was regarded as worth attending one hundred or less years ago unless there was a little playful display with the blackthorn before its close. Indeed, I have it on the best local tradition that there was a general belief amongst the full-blooded men of the time that unless they had a certain amount of blood drawn periodically through the popular medium or otherwise their health would suffer.

Fifty years or so ago between 1st and 15th August pilgrims in quite large numbers, many from a considerable distance, attended to make the stations as it was termed; but to show the changes which time brings about in so many ways, the stations is but a mere shadow of what it was half a century ago.

The Belfast antiquarian Francis Joseph Bigger visited the holy well and was upset when he saw the neglect it had suffered. He wrote a letter to the *Impartial Reporter*, which was published on 11 September 1913:

Vandal minds and destructive hands planned and laid the new road right through the sacred spot, breaking up the old paths and dividing the stations, injuring the well, just as they wished to break the old faith and ancient rites … Surely now, however a better era is dawning and the church of the holy well, the church of St Patrick, will yet be saved as the most sacred and lovely thing in the parish of Cleenish?

Tradition says the old people ignored the church's disapproval and continued to make the stations. They still do today, although not in as great numbers as in the past.

It's a beautiful place, with roots reaching back into Ireland's pagan past. Over the years it has been changed into a Christian site and it is well worth a visit.

Struell Wells

The Stuel Wells are a few miles from Downpatrick Cathedral. (From Downpatrick travel along Edward Street to the Ardglass Road and look for the Struell Road, which is on the left side and travel along it. The wells are signposted. Entrance is free.) The site contains the ruins of a church, two wells and the remains of two bathing houses. Its water, like that of Belcoo Holy Well, is said to have healing properties and the site was once a place of pilgrimage. Protective structures have been placed around Struell Wells. Two bathhouses and a church were also built on the site. Originally the structures were made of woven branches, which were eventually replaced with stone buildings. One of the wells is reputed to cure bad backs. My back's fine so I've never used its waters. The other well is said to cure deteriorating eyesight. I once washed my eyes in it and was convinced my sight did improve. Later I learned that while bathing the eyes one should be praying for spiritual sight and I didn't do that. I just wanted to avoid wearing glasses so I could see more clearly to read. I suspect thinking my sight improved was a placebo effect. Or perhaps increasing light made seeing easier as winter turned into spring? I ended up needing reading glasses about a year later.

There are two ruined bathhouses on the site now, one for men and one for women. The oral history records that originally there was only one bathhouse. Men and women stripped naked and sat together talking. Years later ideas of modesty arrived and it was considered inappropriate for men and women to bathe together, so a special bathhouse was built for women.

I tested the temperature of the water rushing into the women's bathhouse. It was freezing! I was glad not to be living in the past and on a pilgrimage. Putting my hand in the water was bad enough, never mind the whole of my body exposed, naked, to Irish weather and sitting on stone cold seats in freezing water! That's a strange thing about water in holy wells. The temperature deviates from that found in normal wells. It's either warmer or colder – or occasionally, as in the case of St Patrick's Holy Well in Belcoo, it's warm in winter and cold in summer!

St Patrick, the patron Saint of Ireland, was not consistent in his actions. He had a bit of a temper and sometimes cursed places where he'd been annoyed, such as the River Duff. He got rid of all the fish in it because the locals refused to give him any! He must have been in a good mood at Struell because an old folk tale says he was trying to sleep beside the Struell stream when water from it splashed his over beard and surplice, so he blessed the waters and gave them healing properties.

Most holy wells have disappeared, leaving perhaps a record in oral history, as is the case with what's known as 'the wee church' in Seapatrick, which is now part of Banbridge. It's an Anglican church built on a site used by St Patrick as he travelled from Downpatrick to Armagh. He usually went via Newry but sometimes travelled via Seapatrick. The church is situated on the left side of the road going towards Lurgan. The oral tradition states that, except during times of war, a bell has been rung every Sunday on the site since St Patrick walked the earth and that one of the reasons he founded his church there was because there was a well on the site, which has since disappeared. Late local historian Horace Rea decided to take the oral tradition seriously and arranged for an expert water diviner to see if he could find it. He discovered a buried well! The congregation was delighted and the well was uncovered. Unfortunately, Health and Safety insisted it was a danger as somebody might fall in and it was covered. At present a well-like structure marks the spot.

HUNGRY GRASS

Hungry grass is said to be a place where someone died of starvation, probably during a time of famine. Folklore states the horror of the slow death is imprinted on the land, so if anyone walks through a field and enters that space, that person will be overcome by a terrible weakness, become unable to move and may die. I have a friend, who wishes to be anonymous, who told me one day she was walking through a field near Upper Ballinderry where she lived. It was a beautiful day, the birds were singing and she felt happy and well. Suddenly she was overcome with weakness, stumbled and fell. She said:

I've never felt so awful either before, or since. I was terrified as I lay there because I felt I was going to die. Then I remembered about the hungry grass and knew in my bones I was lying on the spot where some poor soul had died. I felt I had to make a big effort to get away. I struggled and managed to move about a metre [3ft] and began to feel better. After several minutes I was fine, although terribly shaken. I was able to enjoy the rest of my walk.

J

IRISH COFFEE

Irish coffee was the brainchild of a man from County Tyrone called Joe Sheridan. He was born in Bridgetown near Castlederg in 1909 and from childhood had a burning ambition to become a chef. During the Second World War he applied for and got a job in Foynes restaurant, which was one of the top establishments in the whole of Ireland. It is in Foynes Airport, a small place in the south of Ireland, near Limerick. As a chef, Joe catered for passengers on early transatlantic flights. The north of Ireland was part of the United Kingdom and played an important part in resisting Hitler during the Second World War. The south referred to the war as 'The Emergency' and remained neutral. Germany didn't always respect that neutrality and attacked it on several occasions, so flying was dangerous. Joe's clients were tired, jet-lagged and frightened. One night during the late winter of 1943 a flight set out from Foynes for Norwood in Newfoundland. The weather was so atrocious the plane's captain decided he'd better turn back to Foynes and hope to start out again in the morning. The passengers were badly shaken and Joe, along with other members of the airport staff, was contacted and asked to make something that would be warm and comforting for them. Pouring whiskey into tea or coffee is an old custom in Ireland and Scotland, so, on the spur of the moment, Joe added a spoonful of sugar to the coffee along with some whiskey and floated cream on top. The passengers really enjoyed their treat and one of them asked, 'Is that Brazilian coffee?' Joe jokingly replied, 'No! It's Irish coffee.' Afterwards he started thinking and the more he thought the more he decided it was a great idea, but the presentation should be improved. Several weeks later he made Irish coffee in a stemmed glass. He thought that looked good and decided to get a second opinion, so he took it to Brendan O'Reagan, the restaurant's owner, and asked what he thought. Brendan said, 'Chef, that's sheer genius. Sheer genius!'

Foynes Airport closed in 1946 and was replaced by Shannon International Airport on the other side of the River Shannon. Joe Sheridan became chief chef in its new restaurant and he made a point of always serving Irish coffee to VIP passengers. In 1952 he moved to Bueno Vista Restaurant in San Francisco and introduced Irish coffee to his customers. He is buried in Oakland, California, and his gravestone is engraved with the words, 'Here lies Joe Sheridan, the inventor of the world's most famous drink, Irish Coffee'. As a result people living in San Francisco believe that Irish coffee originated there! It didn't. It originated in the mind of a man from Bridgetown, near Castlederg in County Tyrone!

It is said that:

The cream is a thick as an Irish brogue,
The coffee is as strong as a friendly hand,
The sugar is as sweet as the tongue of a rogue,
With whiskey as smooth as the wit of the land

IRVINESTOWN'S GARDEN OF CELTIC SAINTS

Once when we were staying in Mahon's Hotel in Irvinestown, the owner, Joe Mahon, suggested we visit the Garden of Celtic Saints, which is in the grounds of the Sacred Heart Church, Lisnarick Road, Irvinestown. Devonish Parish wanted to provide a place of peace and beauty that could be enjoyed by everyone, a place that was fraught with meaning, and not a mere tourist attraction, and the idea of a Garden of Celtic Saints was born. The parish aimed to make a sculpture garden that was a place of beauty and hope, prayer and reflection. They commissioned Jonas Raiskas, a native of Lithuania, to carve statues from native Irish oak. He came to Irvinestown in 2007 and worked until 2011.

The garden is a gem hidden among fir trees. It consists of a series of sculptures protected from the elements by huts. The site also contains statutes depicting Jonas and the whale, and our minds were blown away. It's well worth a visit, and it's free!

We thought the huts looked strange but when we entered one we were immediately entranced. We were surrounded by a lovely sense of spirituality, partly inspired by ethereal music that plays when you enter. We loved the poetry displayed on each hut's walls. Each hut tells its own story. I was particularly interested in the mythology and with the poems said to have been written by saints who have strong connections with County Fermanagh, such as Patrick, Killan, Molaise, Bridgid, Colombanus and Columcille.

The garden succeeds in its aims of providing a place of beauty, hope, reflection and prayer. We felt refreshed by it and we met a woman who lived in Irvinestown. She said:

> My husband died last year. I was in a terrible state. I didn't know which way to turn I don't know what drew me up here but when I arrived I felt a great sense of peace. I felt he was near. Now I come every day and just wander around. I mightn't have time to spare but even a short visit helps me focus on the day and it's such a comfort.

We meant to spend a few minutes there but when we looked at our watches we found several hours had passed. We left with the memory of an old Irish blessing ringing in our minds:

An (1845–48) Old Irish Blessing
May the road rise up to meet you.
May the wind always be at your back.
May the sun shine warm upon your face,
and the rains fall soft upon your fields.
And until we meet again,
May God hold you in the palm of His Hand.

There's a garden commemorating the Great Famine (1845–47) nearby. It is interesting but I was disappointed to find few references to County Fermanagh, which suffered very badly during that time.

J

JACK O'LANTERN

Jack O'Lantern originated from an old Irish folk tale about a very mean man called Stingy Jack. Jack liked the Devil, so he invited him for a drink. When he went to pay for it, the stingy side of his nature came to the fore and he asked the Devil to turn himself into a coin that could be used to pay the bill. Stingy Jack decided to keep the coin and put it into his pocket, along with a silver cross that prevented the Devil changing back to his original shape.

Eventually Stingy Jack must have had an attack of conscience, because he released the Devil on the understanding that he would not be harmed for a year, after which he expected to die. When the year was up Jack tricked the Devil into climbing a tree to pick some fruit. Once the Devil was up the tree Jack decided he didn't want to die, so he carved a cross into the tree's bark that trapped the Devil for ten years, after which Jack died and tried to get into heaven. St Peter saw that Stingy Jack was a bad, mean person who could not be trusted and refused to let him through the pearly gates. The Devil felt sorry for Stingy Jack and gave him a coal to light his way. At that time Irish people ate a lot of turnips. Stingy Jack found a large turnip in a field, carved a face in it and threw the lighted coal inside. He was sometimes seen wandering through the bogs, particularly at Halloween when the dead return to earth to haunt it. When Irish people saw his light they said, 'Oh look! There's Jack of the Lantern.' Over time that changed to Jack O'Lantern and they began to carve lanterns out of turnips. Irish emigrants took the story to America. There weren't any turnips there, so pumpkins were used instead. Eventually pumpkins reached Ireland. They are easier to carve than turnips, so today turnips have been superseded by pumpkins.

JOHN MITCHEL

John Mitchel (1815–75) was either famous or infamous, depending on your viewpoint. He was born near Dungiven in County Londonderry, the son of a Presbyterian minister. He trained as a solicitor and in the year 1840 he obtained a job with Mr Fraser, who had a solicitor's practice in Newry, County Down. The firm expanded and opened premises in Banbridge. John Mitchel was put in charge. He became annoyed because the law was so unfair. People of influence could get off with blue murder while paupers guilty of stealing food were punished severely. He started writing pamphlets and articles attacking the government. In 1848, he started a journal called *The United Irishman*. His writing caused him to be tried for treason, found guilty and transported to Tasmania, where he served fourteen years as a prisoner before escaping and going to South Carolina. He supported slavery during the American Civil War as he thought American slaves were better off than the poor in Ireland. Two of his sons fought in the Civil War, were killed and their graves are in Charleston, South Carolina.

John Mitchel eventually returned to Ireland. He was elected as a Member of Parliament for Tipperary in 1875. However, the election was declared invalid because he was a convicted felon. A by-election was called. Mitchel stood again and was re-elected with an increased majority, which was a great problem for the government! Mitchel then solved the problem by dying of natural causes shortly after the results were declared.

John Mitchel's statue in Newry.

K

KELVIN HOUSE

Kelvin House is a large, modern building containing two blue plaques recording the lives of two men who contributed to past developments in science. It replaced a series of what were originally Georgian dwellings and it is opposite a boys' school, Belfast Academical Institution. The building is named after William Thompson (1824–1907), who later became Lord Kelvin. He was one of the most eminent scientists of the nineteenth century, who devised Kelvin's Law which states that the 'most economical size of a conductor is that for which the annual interest and depreciation on the conductor's capital cost is equal to the annual cost of energy loss'. It can be calculated! Frankly I wish I knew what it means!

William Thompson was born in what is now downtown Belfast in 17 College Square East, opposite Belfast's Academical Institution, locally known as 'Inst'. Originally the street contained a row of elegant, tall Georgian houses. Some of them, including Kelvin's old home, have been redeveloped to form a large single building, Kelvin House.

His father, James Thompson (1789–1846), was born near Ballynahinch, the son of a small farmer. (The house was later called Spamount.) His father educated him at home until he was 10 or 11, then sent him to Samuel Edgar's School at Ballykine near Ballynahinch, where he quickly rose to become an assistant. He wanted to become a Presbyterian church minister, so he entered the University of Glasgow in 1810, studied for several sessions and supported himself by teaching at Ballykine school during the summer. He graduated with an MA in 1812. In 1814 he was appointed teacher of arithmetic, bookkeeping, and geography in Belfast Academical Institution. In 1815 he was professor of mathematics in its collegiate department. He married Margaret Gardner in 1817 and of their children, four boys and two girls survived infancy. William, the future Lord Kelvin, was the couple's fourth child. Margaret died in 1830 when William was 6 years old. His father stepped up to the mark and home educated his two elder sons, William and James, before he sent them to Inst. The younger sons were tutored by their sisters. One sister, Anna, was the mother of physicist James Thomson Bottomley (1845–1926).

James Thompson wrote textbooks on mathematics and was such a good teacher that in 1829 Glasgow University awarded him the honorary degree of LLD. He was appointed Professor of Mathematics to Glasgow University in 1832 and the family moved to the city. He stayed there until he died in 1849.

Lord Kelvin's brother, James Thompson (1822–92), became well known because of his work on water wheels. He was Professor of Engineering at Queen's University Belfast in 1855. In 1873 he became the Regius Professor of Civil Engineering and Mechanics at the University of Glasgow. Thompson introduced a method of deep-sea depth sounding in which a steel piano wire replaces the ordinary hand line. The wire glides so easily to the bottom that 'flying soundings' can be taken while the ship is at full speed. A pressure gauge to register the depth of the sinker was added by Thompson at the University of Glasgow in 1873.

Lord Kelvin was an outstanding mathematician, mathematical physicist and engineer. He was the Professor of Natural Philosophy at the University of Glasgow for fifty-three years and he often worked with his elder brother, James. Physics was in its infancy at the time and he helped to unify it. He undertook research on the mathematical analysis of electricity, discovered the first and second laws of thermodynamics and was involved with laying the first transatlantic cable. He was a keen yachtsman who became dissatisfied with the compasses in use at the time so he developed a more accurate one.

Lord Kelvin worked on the measurement of temperature. At the time there were two temperature scalens in use: Centigrade (now also known as Celsius), and Fahrenheit. Celsius, the one normally used as standard, places the freezing point of water at 0 degrees and its boiling point at 100 degrees, while Fahrenheit places the freezing point of water at -32 degrees and the boiling point at 212 degrees. All substances are made of atoms joined together in different ways to make molecules. Although we aren't aware of it, these molecules are always moving. If they move very quickly they turn into steam. That's the boiling point. As the molecules become colder and colder they move slower and slower. Lord Kelvin discovered that molecules stop moving at -273C or -459F. The units he used to measure temperature above this 'absolute' zero are called Kelvins (K) in his honour. He called freezing point 0K while the boiling point is 373.15K.

Another thermodynamic process, the Joule–Thompson effect, is also named after him (also called the Joule–Kelvin or Kelvin–Joule effect). It describes what happens when a real gas or liquid is forced through a valve or porous plug effect while being kept from losing heat through insulation. That's called a throttling or

Joule–Thompson process. Most liquids, such as hydraulic oils, are warmed by this process. It is used to remove heat from fridges, or applied the other way around, in heat exchangers.

Lord Kelvin was awarded the following prizes: First Smith's Prize (1845), Royal Medal (1856), Keith Medal (1864), Matteucci Medal (1876), Albert Medal (1879), and Copley Medal (1883). He was elected to the Royal Society in 1851 and was its president from 1890 to 1895. In 1892 William Thompson became the first scientist to be elevated to the House of Lords. He chose to become Lord Kelvin because of his connection with Glasgow. He died in 1907 and was buried in Westminster Abbey, and there is a modern memorial to him beside his father's grave on the northern slopes of the Glasgow Necropolis to the east of the main bridge entrance. He is remembered in Belfast by the blue plaque marking the position of the place of his birth and by a large bronze statue by the well-known Belfast sculptor Albert Bruce Joy in Belfast's beautiful Botanic Gardens.

The other blue plaque on Kelvin House celebrates the life of Robert Shipboy McAdam (1805–95), a Presbyterian who made an important contribution to the cultural life of Belfast. He was a major commissioner and collector of the Irish language. A lot of his material now belongs to Belfast's Linen Hall Library.

L

LAMBEG DRUMS

Lambeg drums get their name from the village of Lambeg in County Antrim, which was originally about 9 miles to the south of Belfast. It has been swallowed by the Belfast/Lisburn conurbation. The drums were huge, noisy instruments of war. They measure approximately 3ft ¼in (92.1cm) in diameter, 2ft (61cm) in depth and weigh between 35 and 40lb (16–18kg). They were designed to scare the living daylights out of the enemy. Today they are associated with traditional parades, notably by those organised by the Protestant Orange Order but also the Foresters, who organise St Patrick's parades. Jack Johnston, who lives in Cloghher, says that in his youth a Lambeg drum was decorated with shamrocks for the Catholic St Patrick Day parades and the same drum wore orange lilies

Lambeg drums.

when it was needed for a Protestant parade! Unfortunately a lot of polarisation occurred during the recent Troubles so such co-operation is not as common as it once was. In the past a strong man who was built like, to use the local parlance, a brick s**t house, carried the drum. He paraded for miles and was usually accompanied by a very small man playing a flute. The pair were a comical sight. Today the drummers are more likely to be found beating the life out of a drum in what had been a quiet corner on the parade route before it began. Several strong men take it in turns to play the instrument.

LANGUAGE

The language spoken in Northern Ireland is unique. Sometimes it makes strangers feel alarmed. For example, if you go into a café, or a restaurant, and the waitress asks, 'Would you like a wee bite?' that doesn't mean she's offering to bite you. A 'bite' can mean something to eat, so 'Would you like a wee bite?' means 'Would you like something to eat?' 'Wee' is a very common word. It's been said that 'everything's wee', although that doesn't mean it is necessarily small! You may spend a fortune and be asked, 'Would you like a wee bill?' and find it costs a fortune. I love it when my hairdresser says, 'I can do your wee hair on Tuesday at 10.30'. Another of my favourites is 'wee small', as in 'He's just a wee small man'.

The word 'wee' can be very confusing, as in 'wee buns'. That doesn't necessarily mean small cakes, it could also mean it was very easy, as in 'that exam was wee buns!' or 'she's a bun in the oven', meaning she's pregnant, which can also be described as 'up the bubble'.

Another peculiar phrase, usually at the beginning of a sentence, is 'see me', 'see her', 'see him'. Once in a queue in a supermarket I heard a woman say to a friend, 'See me? See my man? See cheese? Can't stand it!' I surmised from that neither she nor her husband liked cheese!

'See me' isn't always used in a negative context. You may hear something like, 'See me? See Majorkey? Love it!', which means 'I love Majorca!'

Malapropisms are common, especially in areas such as Belfast's Shankill Road, where you may hear phrases such as, 'She was turrible bad. She had to have a sectarian operation', meaning 'She had such a difficult time during labour she had to have a Caesarian operation'. I think my favourite is, 'She had a hysterical rectum!' meaning 'She had a hysterectomy!'

Some phrases that are often added on to the end of a sentence are: 'so it is', 'so I am', 'so I do', 'so we are' and 'so they are', as in, 'It's raining, so it is', 'I'm fed up, so I am!', 'I think that's right, so I do!', 'We're off on holiday tomorrow, so we are' and 'Our politicians are useless, so they are!'

Anything that is excellent is said to be 'dead on'. It's a very common phrase. Literally anything can be described as 'dead on', as in 'thon meal was dead on', 'thon movie's dead on', 'he's dead on', 'there's a dead on show in the Opera House'. When Harland and Wolff Shipyard was changing owners, prospective owners asked a workman if he was used to working very accurately. The workman replied indignantly, 'Sir, we have to be dead on!'

Another way of saying something's excellent is to say 'it's class', as in 'it's a class place', or 's/he's class'.

'Bout ye?' is another common phrase that's a shortened version of 'How's about ye?', which can mean either 'hello' or 'how are you'.

'Craic', pronounced 'crack', can cause confusion. 'Craic' means 'fun', so if somebody asks, 'Do you feel some craic', you're not being asked if you'd like cocaine! It simply means 'would you like some fun?' 'Quare craic' means very good fun, as in 'it was quare craic', and 'the 'craic was mighty' means it was outstanding fun.

'Keep her lit' means keep a mental spark going. The phrase has nothing to do with a fire, although poets, musicians or other creative people may be encouraged during Eureka moments with comments such as 's/he's on fire!'

One of my favourite sayings is 'It was giv out!', as in 'It was giv out that it was going to rain.'

By the way, people who are native to Northern Ireland call their country 'Norn Iron'!

LEAP OF THE DOG AND LIMAVADY

Limavady is a market town situated on the River Roe 17 miles east of Derry/Londonderry. It's in a beautiful situation, with Binevenagh as a backdrop. It has a curious name derived from Irish, Léim an Mhadaidh (the leap of the dog), which changed over time to Limavady. No one is sure of the exact date of Limavady's origin. Estimates suggest about AD 5 and early records say that St Columba held a meeting of the kings at Mullagh Hill near Limavady in AD 575. The site is now part of the Roe Valley Resort.

In ancient times the land around Limavady belonged to the O'Cahan family. Sir Thomas Phillips was granted 13,000 acres of land, including the O'Cahan castle, during the plantation of Ulster and he built 'Newtown of Limavady', which was laid out in a cruciform pattern. The old name Léim an Mhadaidh was anglicised to Limavady. The story behind the name is part of the O'Cahan family history. According to local myth, the O'Cahans suffered a surprise attack from their enemies. They had a much-loved family dog, who leapt from O'Cahan's Rock in Roe Park right across the River Roe and managed to summon help. Its feat has gone down in history, having been incorporated in the town's name.

I have a particular affection for Limavady because during the Troubles I attended the christening of my great-niece, Georgiana Mason, in a Presbyterian

The Leap of the Dog. (Printed with kind permission of Anne McMaster)

church in Limavady. We were coming from Banbridge and in those days it was advisable to leave a lot of spare travel time to allow for possible checkpoints, bomb scares and so on. (I would like to stress Northern Ireland has a very low crime rate. Even counting the Troubles it was amongst the lowest in Europe!) We had a pleasant, trouble-free journey, were very early, found the church, parked outside and dandered up the street and round the corner looking for somewhere to have a cup of coffee. We found what looked like a pub. The door was open. We walked in and saw a girl sitting reading a newspaper. We asked if we could have a cup of coffee. She said, 'Sure!' She made us one and served it in mismatched mugs and continued reading the paper. We thought her behaviour was a bit strange. We finished our coffee and asked her for a bill. She smiled and said, 'There is no charge. We're shut and we don't serve coffee!'

LINEN HALL LIBRARY

The Linen Hall Library developed from Belfast Reading Society. It was established on 13 May 1788. It's opposite Belfast's City Hall, physically in the centre of Belfast and at the centre of the cultural and creative life of the wider community. It's an independent and charitable body, the oldest library in Northern Ireland and the last subscribing library. In 1795 it passed a resolution stating, 'The object of this Society is the collection of an extensive library, philosophical apparatus and such products of nature and art as tend to improve the mind and excite a spirit of general enquiry.'

The Linen Hall Library is a wonderful place. It's full of books and a sense of being steeped in history. At times it has struggled with finance, so in 1980 it was decided to accept some public funding and encourage public access to its collections. It has interesting collections concentrating on Irish studies, politics and culture. Its collections include information on early Belfast and Ulster printed books, periodicals and newspapers dating back as far as 1738, and comprehensive archives including maps, materials in the Irish language, and an archive of the recent Troubles with material on all sides of the conflict. Its strength is broadmindedness and acceptance of different viewpoints. One of its early committee members, Henry Joy McCracken, was hanged for treason in 1794 because at that time Catholics and all Protestants who did not belong to the established (Anglican) Church were forbidden education and certain civil rights. He was involved, with other Presbyterians and many Catholics, in the 1798 rebellion.

LISSAN HOUSE

Lissan House is full of happy ghosts! It's a beautiful 400-year-old house in County Tyrone situated about 2 miles north of Cookstown. It's just off the B162 Draperstown/Lough Fea Road, in the heart of Glenkonkeyne, an ancient wooded district bathed in enchantment. It's densely wooded and the area is thought to have been used for religious and ceremonial purposes in the past.

The house was home to the Staples family, who were part of the Plantation of Ulster. The original building dates from about 1620. Hazel Radclyffe-Dolling (née Staples) was the last occupant. She died in April 2006 and so Lissan House homed the longest-known occupation of a domestic dwelling by a single family in Northern Ireland. Now it is open to the public and it's well worth a visit.

The story begins with an adventurous, enterprising young barrister called Thomas Staples. He was born near Bristol at Yate Court. Around 1610 he decided to go to Ireland and make a new life. He settled in Moneymore, a town that was being built as part of the terms of the Plantation Grant to the Worshipful Company of Drapers. In other words, it is a Plantation house, marked on a Thomas Raven map of 1622 beside the Market Cross. Thomas Staples built his house from timber, stone and handmade bricks. He set up an ironworks, felling great oaks for charcoal to smelt the ore. It was a very happy house with inhabitants who were reluctant to leave it when they died, so it has become regarded as the most haunted house in the north of Ireland.

King Charles I created Thomas Staples 1st Baronet of Lissan and Faughanvale in 1628. His descendants lived here through times of poverty and prosperity, conflict and peace, over four centuries. The Staples family grew and flourished through time, contributing significantly to the local community, the Church, business and the Crown. Dr Neil Watt, a past manager of the house, is a very level-headed young man who told me he definitely did not believe in ghosts until he came to work in Lissan in 2019. He said:

> At Christmas I worked hard all day collecting holly and ivy to use as decorations and I became starving with hunger. I wanted to finish what I was doing to I phoned my sister and asked if she'd bring me a Chinese takeaway. Now she's very sensible, down to earth and definitely not the sort with an overindulgent imagination. She drove up the driveway, parked the car, came into the house and asked, 'Why didn't you say you'd company? I'd have brought two takeaways?' Neil said he didn't have company, she replied, 'You're joking! I saw a podgy young man, dressed in tweeds, standing beside the piano, chatting away to you.' She was shocked when I told her there was nobody there!

Once, when Neil was working in the ballroom, he heard a dog barking at his feet. There was a definite, 'Woof! Woof', the kind of excited bark a dog emits when it wants to be taken for a walk, yet there was no dog there. Neil said:

> I did something I never thought I'd do in my wildest dreams. I asked a medium to come to Lissan. She asked me if I liked dogs. I told her I do and asked her how she knew. She replied, 'Because there are two dogs running around your feet, a terrier and a red setter.'

On another occasion, Neil and one of the trustees were setting up a piano in the ballroom, and they heard two ladies laughing. When Neil went on an errand to the far end of the house, the trustee heard chitter-chatter behind him, although there was nobody there.

One night, the burglar alarm went off. The chairman came to turn it off and check the premises. He walked from room to room, and as he reached Lady Staples' bedroom something attacked him and knocked him down. Neil asked a medium to come in and tell him what was going on:

> She said Alexander Staples, who was a founder member of the family, loved the house he built and his spirit stayed to look after it. He was particularly protective of Lady Staples' bedroom and was standing shaking his fists and shouting obscenities at them. She said, 'The best way to deal with a ghost is to face it. Whenever you feel Alexander's presence, talk to him. Tell him you love his old home. You'd never harm it. It needs to be looked after so you are only taking care of it.' Whenever I go near Lady Staples bedroom I always talk to Alexander. I feel a right eejit, but I haven't had any trouble with him.

Mrs Hazel Radcliffe Dolling, the last family member who owned the house, used Lady Staples' bedroom as a guest room. Women sleeping there often said they had heard footsteps during the night and sometimes a lady wearing a gold dress, carrying a doll and a lighted candle, would come into the room and try to set fire to the bed. Neil wonders if she's the reason Alexander Staples is protective of Lady Staples' old bedroom?

Hazel Radcliffe Dolling spent the last years of her life living alone in Lissan House. She died in 2006 at the ripe old age of 82. She had many strange tales to tell about ghostly goings on around the old house. Sometimes she'd hear heavy footsteps that sounded like those of a man yet there was nobody there. At times she smelt lavender or rose petals, or heard the sobs of a small child. Once a visitor saw children playing noisily in the hall. She turned to ask them who they were, but they skipped off down the hall and vanished into thin air. Hazel was asked if she was frightened living with so many ghosts? She said, 'No! Why should I be? I'm just surrounded by my family. They would never hurt me and they keep me company. I'm never really alone.'

The ghost of a very shy little girl, about 11 or 12 years of age, has frequently been seen by people walking in the gardens. She looks out of one of the windows on the top floor and she has been photographed, although there's nobody there!

Sir Thomas Staples, 9th Baronet (31 July 1775–14 May 1865), was an Anglo-Irish politician and lawyer and was one of the wealthiest men in Ireland. He inherited Lissan House in the mid-nineteenth century. He added the ballroom and hired an orchestra to live permanently with his family. He and his family divided their time between County Tyrone and their mansion in Dublin's Merrion Square. He had a very beautiful wife, Lady Catherine Staples, known as handsome Kitty Staples. She loved music, entertaining and spending money. Her husband died many years before her and as she'd been unable to have children the estate passed to her nephew, Nathaniel Staples, a penniless civil servant, who lived in India. When Nathaniel and Lady Kitty met they hated each other! She moved out of the house, taking all the furniture, doors and light fittings with her, so her nephew was left with an empty shell. Her actions annoyed the ghosts living there because they loved their old home and didn't like seeing it destroyed, so she's not a happy ghost. It is said that her actions brought bad luck to the family, causing them to lose a lot of money and the high place they once occupied in society.

Lady Staples had her portrait painted by renowned British artist Martin Cregan in 1825. Nathaniel had to sell it in 1898, along with contents from Lissan House, as he needed the money. The trustees of Lissan House managed to raise sufficient money to buy the portrait and bring it back home. They hung it on the drawing room wall and the moment it was put in place Nathaniel's portrait fell on the floor. There was no reason for this. The hooks on the wall remained in place and it was hung by secure wires that were undisturbed. The dislike the couple had for each other must persist beyond the grave.

I think Sir Robert Ponsonby Staples,

'Me? Scared of the ghosts? No! Sure they're just members of my family!'

the bare-footed baronet, is one of the most interesting past owners of Lissan House. Sir Robert was the third son of Sir Nathaniel Staples. He was born in Lissan House in 1853, studied art and architecture from the age of 12 and taught art in London from 1897. He drew political cartoons and his many works include a triptych illustrating Belfast's shipbuilding industry. Many of his drawings and paintings are on display in Lissan House. He played an increasing part in running the house from 1905 and took up residence there in 1910, although he did not inherit the estate, and the baronetcy, until his older brother died in 1933. Sir Robert lived in various addresses around the Knock area in East Belfast before he inherited the Lissan estate and his son went to Campbell College. He died in 1943.

Sir Robert was eccentric. He disliked shoes intensely. He said wearing them kept the healing magnetism from rising out of the earth to keep people healthy and that much of the illness present in the population was caused by wearing shoes. Visitors to Lissan House had to leave their shoes at the door. When he visited London he walked along the tramlines with bare feet to benefit from the metal. He must have looked a strange sight prancing along the tramlines in places like Piccadilly Circus!

M

MATCHMAKERS, MARRIAGE AND MOUNTAINY FOLK

In the past, when young people were strictly supervised, it could be difficult to meet someone of the opposite sex. That was where a matchmaker came in. They have been widely depicted in movies about past life in Ireland. It was their job to find young people suitable partners and introduce them under sufficiently chaste circumstances. The man usually took them for a ride in his pony and trap, which personally I would have found both inhibiting and embarrassing! He negotiated the bride's price and was paid for his services.

Michael J. Murphy, the folklorist, described how once he was in danger of being trapped by a matchmaker when he went for a bicycle ride and ended up in the small town of Carrickmore in County Tyrone. It was Fair Day and he saw the local matchmaker watching the crowd haggle over the price of a cow. The matchmaker looked at Michael and asked, 'Are you for home?' Michael admitted he was and the matchmaker said, 'Ride on a bit, then wait until I catch up with you.' The matchmaker hurried into a pub while Michael did as he was asked. He cycled several miles out of town and sat down on a wall to wait. The matchmaker, who was not far behind him, said, 'I've a bit of a tedious mission.' Michael immediately understood the 'tedious mission' was making matches between two people, who sometimes hardly knew of each other's existence. Eventually a car drove up and stopped. The matchmaker got to his feet and pretended to be lighting his pipe while carefully observing a woman and a girl getting out of it. He eyed the girl and said to Michael, 'No lark's legs yonder. Yon one should be able to stand a bit of abuse!' A basket and some parcels were taken out of the car, which drove off while the woman and the matchmaker walked along talking about the fair, weather, crops and everything unconnected to matchmaking. As he was talking the matchmaker kept watching the girl, who had her eyes fixed firmly on the ground. She must have found the situation embarrassing! The matchmaker asked several questions about her, such as her age, and was told that she was, 'quare and useful around the house'. When the girl looked at Michael, he heard the matchmaker tell the mother what she wanted 'was a decent man, no one

Mountainy folk.

to call at his door for tuppence, sound of limb and mind, with no encumbrances'. He felt the hairs on the back of his neck rise in fear. He jumped on his bike, waved goodbye and rode up the hill as fast as he could go! In retrospect he was very glad to have escaped because the matchmaker found a partner for the girl that day and Michael felt he might have been bullied into marrying her!

In the past, mountainy men lived in isolated communities. Neighbours helped each other by lending implements, joining forces to use their horses in a ploughing team, helping bringing in the harvest and in 'spud hoking' (potato gathering). Women and children helped in that dirty, backbreaking work. Even today school attendance drops during the potato-gathering season as so many schools close for a week around Halloween. Farm life was much more social than it is today as machinery has replaced workers.

I was very lucky to meet Frankie Bradley in a cafe in Gortin. He said he was born into a large family of mountainy folk before the Second World War. He told me mountainy folk lived in isolated places such as the Sperrin Mountains, the Mournes and so on. Frankie said,:

> Life was very hard before the Labour government introduced the National Health Service, free education and unemployment benefit. I remember my mother used

> to make a huge fry for breakfast using several inches of animal fat and huge amounts of homemade bread, bacon and eggs. People were very active in those days and nobody either knew or cared about cholesterol. For dinner my mother boiled a mountain of potatoes, drained the pot in which they were cooked, placed a clean cloth on top of it and poured the potatoes on it. The family sat round the table and helped themselves. My father always helped himself to a massive amount of potatoes, put a lump of butter on top of them and devoured the lot!

Mountainy men were determined to find a wife to give practical help around the farm. Life was so tough there wasn't any room for romance. There's a story about a mountainy man whose wife died. When a neighbour sympathised with him, he said, 'Aye! She was a good catch, indeed and sowl. She was a hard worker and we'd a brave spell together, the guts of sixty years, but do ye know something? I never did like yon woman of mine!'

Marriage was a practical necessity, a wife with a broad back who could pull a plough and who could carry two buckets of water was what mountainy men aimed to find! You were giving your wife great praise if you said, 'Yon woman of mine's so tall she could ate hay out of a loft, like a horse.' Frankie said, 'A pretty face and a good figure were looked upon as a bonus, but they weren't necessary attributes for marriage.'

Regarding wooing, there were two types of Mountainy Men. One was the type that had the gift of the gab, who could sweet-talk a woman from now till kingdom come. If she said, 'Yes', he underwent a shocking metamorphosis. Then there was the sort who took a more practical approach by asking questions like, 'Would you like to be buried with my folk?' or, 'Your land is next to mine. If we married and joined the farms we could make a better livelihood.' That type of attitude is beautifully summed up in the hit song, 'I've Got a Brand-New Combine Harvester'!

Frankie said, 'You didn't have a lot of choice when looking for a wife. The only way of getting anywhere was by your own efforts by either walking of cycling. That narrowed the field somewhat!'

Mountainy men never made 'dates'. They went for 'a scud of a curt' or 'a set' and you talked about 'your hoult'. If a boy appeared at the gate or home of a girl he was half married already.

Once she was married the bride had to prove herself. The reputation of her family depended on her working hard and even hired girls had to work in the fields. At the beginning of the twentieth century it became impossible to make a living on a small farm. During the spring the women helped the men to plough or dig, preparing the land for crops. Once the oats were sown and potatoes planted, the men left to earn money elsewhere, usually working as navvies in England. The mountainy women attended the crops, pigs, poultry and cattle while looking after their families and caring for any old folk who might still be around. The men didn't return until harvest time. Young boys were advised never to work for a woman because she didn't know what a day's work was. That was true. She had to combine the work of two or three days into one.

Any profits from the land belonged to the men but the wife was allowed to make money on her own behalf. She looked after hens, killed fowl and sold them along with surplus eggs. If she had a dairy, she took great pride in it. The floor was washed every day with clean water, earthenware crocks, jars and wooden vessels were scrubbed, and churns, working troughs, rollers, paddles and butter prints were kept spotlessly clean and proudly displayed. Milk pans were placed on cool slabs. The wife probably had only one cow and a small dash churn, which would have catered for her family's butter needs with a few pounds left over to sell.

Women tended to die young as they became worn out by hard work and childbirth, so it was common for a man to have several wives. Hence, girls marrying older men was a common practice. Frankie said, 'My mother was only 18 when she married my father. He was 37.'

Mountainy women were tough and determined to produce good-living, honest, hard-working children. Frankie said that even after he'd grown up, if his mother found he'd sneaked off to enjoy a 'wee smoke' she fetched a blackthorn stick and 'blattered' him with it. It's said mountainy women kept the marriage rate low because they acted as a deterrent.

The Land Act came into force at the beginning of the twentieth century. Until then the land was owned by landlords and was rented out to tenant farmers, who could be evicted without cause. If a tenant farmer made any improvements, they could be taken into account when valuing the land and cause unfair rent rises. At that time people married young. When a mountainy woman owned the land, the marriage of a son mattered in a big material way because it took support away from the farm. Mothers made comments such as, 'He goes and marries, just as we were getting our heads above water!' She'd very readily give her daughter away, but God help any other mother's daughter who wanted to marry her son!

Children were expected to work hard around the farm. Work was mixed with play both before and after school. Scholarship wasn't valued; it didn't help in earning a living on the farm. Children were expected to work hard and focus on the task in hand. If a lad lifted his head while working in a field somebody would have guldered (shouted), 'Is it counting the crows ye are?'

I have direct experience of mountainy people through a distant relation of my husband. When I became engaged I was taken to meet my fiancé's great-aunt Aggie, who lived in a remote cottage near Ahoghill (pronounced A-hock-ill) in County Antrim, in a one-room unconverted cottage. I was told it was important to impress her as she was very influential within the family. When the big day arrived, I made a real effort with my appearance. To put it on local parlance, I made sure I was 'right up the oxters' (armpits).

Aunt Aggie gave me a piercing stare, made me welcome and found me a seat beside the fire between two ancient men, who were smoking clay pipes and gossiping. I was offered a 'wee cup of tea in my hand' (that means it was given to me by the fireside, not sitting at a table). It was poured from a kettle stewing on a crook and crane over the fire. I looked at it doubtfully. It appeared and smelt poisonous. Manfully I drank it. Its concentrated tannin damaged my tonsils and scraped the tartar off my teeth. One of my fiancé's cousins appeared at the door and my fiancé, in the way of all men who are desperately needed, disappeared with him 'to see the cows'.

The fire began to smoke and I started to cough. Aunt Aggie took me outside to escape 'the stour'. We had a really nice conversation about herbs and I was particularly interested in the tansy she had growing outside her door. She told me it kept the flies away, and I told her I'd never seen one in person before but had read that a couple of tansy leaves were nice in a white sauce. Aunt Aggie said she'd try that the next time she was making one. Then she said 'I'm worried 'cos I'm not as steady on my feet as I used to be. I'm frightened of falling off my bicycle when I go to collect my groceries. I was thinking of buying myself a tricycle. What do you think of that?' She was 86 at the time. I told her I thought she was marvellous and a tricycle would be a very good idea, provided she was strong enough to deal with the extra weight. She said she was as she could still do her own housework and 'hoke potatoes'. At this point I became very upset because I could hear the old men discussing me. They said they could see 'poor George was smitten with yon wee girl', 'thon's an awful cough that'll probably kill her. It sounds like consumption', 'she's too wee to be useful' and 'poor George should catch himself on and get himsel' a big useful woman – never mind her face and figure!'

I felt distressed and looked at Aunt Aggie. What did she think? She gave my arm a quick squeeze and said:

> Never mind them two auld fools. They don't know their arses from their elbows. Thon's auld-fashioned talk. You live in a different age from what they

> did. Look at me. I'm small like you! Small ones are wiry. They last. I had a big, sauncy friend. She had a big broad back and she's been dead for years! Them two auld fools can't move with the times. They haven't even got the sense to take their own advice. Both of them took their dead end trying to get me to marry them, but I'd more sense. I've got my own wee home and a wee bit of land so I didn't need them. I'm independent! They used to fight over me but over the years they've made friends and are more interested in each other than in me. They come every afternoon and waste my time by cluttering up my kitchen. And I'll tell you something else. They haven't the guts to drink a decent cup of tea and you finished it!

Aunt Aggie did buy herself a tricycle. She lived until well into her 90s and told the family I was the only one in the family who had 'a bit of sense, as I thought a tricycle was a good idea'. I could see 'being independent's important', and what if it did 'cost a wheen of money' to get the blacksmith to make her one? 'There're no pockets in a shroud.' 'You can't take it with you when you go, so to hell with poverty, put another pea in the soup!' She was my idea of the perfect mountainy woman.

Mountainy living was tough but in many ways it's a pity mountainy people have died out. Their disappearance was caused by the advent of television, improved roads and public transport, better education and job opportunities. They were self-sufficient, hard-working resilient, and caring.

N

NOMADIC

SS *Nomadic* and SS *Traffic* were two tender ships to the ill-fated RMS *Titanic* and her sister ship RMS *Olympic*. They were built in Harland and Wolff's Shipyard in Belfast. Like *Titanic*, the tenders were designed by Thomas Andrews and had the same luxurious finishes. *Nomadic*'s keel was laid down by Harland and Wolff in 1910 (yard number 422). She was built on slipway No. 1 alongside *Olympic* and *Titanic*, which were constructed on slipways 2 and 3, of the Arrol Gantry, respectively. *Nomadic* was launched on 25 April 1911 and delivered to the White Star Line on 27 May, following sea trials. Thanks to the efforts of the Nomadic Preservation Society, the French Titanic Society, Belfast Industrial Heritage, Belfast Titanic Society and the Save Nomadic appeal the tender has come home to Belfast and can be visited in Harland Dock, which is near the Titanic Museum in the Titanic Quarter of East Belfast.

The Titanic Museum.

Nomadic was one quarter of the size of *Titanic*. It was constructed of steel with riveted hull plating, steel frames, beams, bulkheads. There were four working decks with various hold spaces beneath, and when fully loaded the vessel could carry up to 1,000 passengers. Her job was to transfer first- and second-class passengers from the shallow dockside in Cherbourg out to *Titanic* moored in deeper water just off shore.

Passenger accommodation consisted of lower- and upper-deck passenger lounges and open deck areas on the bridge and flying bridge decks. The vessel was divided into first- and second-class passenger areas, with first-class passengers enjoying the fore areas of the ship. There was a small area in the aft end of the lower deck used for overspill of third-class passengers from *Traffic*.

Nomadic was beautiful, especially her first-class section. She was fitted out in the same luxurious fashion as *Olympic* and *Titanic*, with more luxuries than the majority of tenders at the time. She had ornate decorative joinery and plasterwork, particularly in the first-class lounges. There were tables, cushioned benches, porcelain, fine china and water fountains at the fore end of the ship. There was a buffet bar and sex-specific bathrooms.

Nomadic arrived in Cherbourg on 3 June 1911 to begin its tendering duties for White Star. On 10 April 1912 it transported 274 passengers to *Titanic* for its disastrous maiden voyage, including American journalist and United States Army officer Archibald Butt, the Denver millionairess Margaret Brown, mining tycoon Benjamin Guggenheim, New York millionaire John Jacob Astor IV with his new wife Madeleine and their dog Kitty, an Airedale, and Ann Elizabeth Isham with her Great Dane.

The weather was very rough and the sea was so choppy the gangway swayed like mad. Several men did their best to hold it steady, but even so a woman fell and twisted her ankle. The Astors, Ann Elizabeth Isham and their dogs got across safely. There were twelve dogs on *Titanic* when she famously sank during the night of 12 April 1912 after hitting an iceberg, but only three survived – a Pekinese and two Pomeranians. They were so small they could be carried. Ann Elizabeth Isham went down with the ship rather than leave her dog behind. It was too big to go in a lifeboat.

Nomadic continued serving the White Star Line until it was requisitioned by the French government to serve as an auxiliary minesweeper and ferry American troops to and from the harbour in Brest, France. After the war, it went back to tendering duties. It was sold to the Compagnie Cherbourgeoise de Transborde-ment (CCT) in 1927 and continued to act as tender under its new ownership.

In 1934 the White Star and Cunard Line made *Nomadic* redundant by merging and opening an enlarged port at Cherbourg that could accommodate large ships. It was sold to the Société Cherbourgeoise de Sauvetage et de Remorquage (SCSR or Cherbourg Tow & Rescue Society) and renamed *Ingenieur Minard*.

During the Second World War, *Ingenieur Minard* took part in the evacuation of Cherbourg on 18 June 1940. Then it was requisitioned by the Royal Navy and based in Portsmouth harbour, where it operated as an accommodation ship.

During the war the Cherbourg port was heavily damaged, so large ocean liners couldn't dock there. *Ingenieur Minard* was saved from the shipbreakers and after the war returned to tendering duties for the SCSR from Cherbourg. It took passengers to ocean liners such as *Queen Mary* and *Queen Elizabeth*, and finally retired on 4 November 1968. It then lay idle for five years before being bought by a private individual, Yvon Vincent, who changed the name back to *Nomadic*, and on 26 April 1969 it was moved to Le Havre and converted into a floating restaurant and function vessel. In October 1974, *Nomadic* was relocated to the River Seine near the Eiffel Tower in Paris. The owners were faced with financial difficulties in 1999 and the ship was seized by Paris harbour authorities in 2002. On 1 April 2002 it was towed out of Paris. Some superstructure had to be removed because there had been changes on the Seine and it could not have been towed under the new lower bridges. On 1 April 2002 *Nomadic* arrived in Le Havre, where an attempt was made to find a buyer. If a buyer wasn't forthcoming, the ship was at risk being sold for scrap. That would have been a shame as it is the last surviving ship built by the famous White Star Line, never mind its *Titanic* connection. On hearing of its threatened fate, heritage and maritime enthusiasts (including the newly set up Nomadic Preservation Society) began raising the money to buy the vessel. The campaigns were well supported by the public, particularly those in Northern Ireland, but they were unable to raise sufficient funds to meet *Nomadic*'s reserve price. Fortunately the price was lowered and the campaigns gained political and governmental support, including from the French. On 26 January 2006, the Northern Ireland government Department for Social Development paid £263,000,000 at auction.

Bringing *Nomadic* home was a nightmare! It was so rusted it was in danger of sinking, so it was tethered to another ship to keep it afloat and they were pulled by tugs. Luckily the weather co-operated and everyone breathed a sigh of relief when it arrived in Belfast and the job of renovation could begin. Some members of the Nomadic Preservation Society found a lot of the original panelling in a restaurant in Paris, and one of the two lifeboats was found in Belgium. The other was in such a bad state it was beyond redemption.

The restoration process had some hair-raising moments. Workers on *Nomadic* became aware of a presence when one night two men, working in the bowels of the ship, heard a man and a women talking and dogs barking. There was nobody there. Their hair stood on end and a shiver shimmied up their spines! What happened to the two dogs that travelled on *Nomadic*? Kitty's body was never found. John Jacob Astor's body was so mangled by the propeller he was identified by his gold watch. His wife survived because he put her in a lifeboat. Ann Elizabeth Isham's body was discovered with her arms around her Great Dane.

Nomadic is now a tourist attraction. It may be visited in Hamilton Dock, Belfast, near the Titanic Museum.

O

OLD INN CRAWFORDSBURN

There was an ancient highway between the priory at Holywood (that's how Holywood gets its name – Holy Wood) and its parent abbey at Bangor.

Crawfordsburn lies between Holywood and Bangor, so it made a good stopping point, which led to the establishment of a hostelry before the advent of modern transport. The village of Crawfordsburn grew up around the Old Inn. Crawfordsburn is a delightful place with whitewashed cottages and craft shops.

Nobody knows when an inn was established. It probably dates back to very early times, possibly to the establishment of nearby Christian institutions. What is known is that the Old Crawfordsburn Inn was founded in 1600, at the end of Queen Elizabeth I's reign. Records show the Old Inn was in its present form around 1614. There's evidence of substantial additions made during the middle of the eighteenth century. They involved some of the upstairs bedrooms and the kitchen. The east wing is modern, based on Irish Georgian style.

The Old Inn takes pride in owning a quern grindstone carved with the sign of the cross. It's in the corridor leading to the bar. It came from Bangor's ancient abbey and originally belonged to one of the students. The students had to grind their own meal supply as part of the discipline to which they were subjected. (Bangor Castle and Bangor Abbey have preserved many other treasures from the past.)

The Old Inn was used by smugglers right up to the end of the eighteenth century, with secret hiding places for contraband still being found well into the twentieth century!

The mail coach that connected with the sailing ship changed horses at the Old Inn. As a result, the Tzar of Russia, Peter the Great, stayed there when he toured Ulster studying developments in the manufacture of damask linen, a textile for which the province is renowned. Many famous writers, such as Anthony Trollope, Dean Swift, Charles Dickens, William Makepeace Thackeray and Alfred, Lord Tennyson, have also been residents. In 1958 C.S. Lewis (see later) and his wife Joy spent a belated honeymoon there, having what they described as 'a perfect fort-night'.

American visitors are particularly interested to hear that Paul Jones stayed in the Old Inn, as did the famous highwayman Dick Turpin. He had to flee from England and spent his exile in Crawfordsburn. On a more serious note, part of King William III's army marched through the village on their way from Groomsport to join the main forces at Belfast.

OSCAR WILDE AND OTHER WRITERS

Oscar Wilde was born in Dublin on 16 October 1854, the second son of two very gifted parents, and was sent to school in Northern Ireland. His father, Sir William Wilde, was a well-known and well-liked character in Dublin. He was a surgeon, an archaeologist and an auralist, who 'liked other women'! Apparently he 'was never really drunk but never sober'. His mother, Lady Wilde, was an ardent Irish Nationalist with a life-long interest in Irish folk tales, which she had published. She also wrote poetry under the pen name Speranza. That was very wise because she, like John Mitchel, disapproved of the actions of the British government during the Great Famine and she would have been taken to court and tried for treason if her identity had been revealed. Democracy and free speech have developed since the 1800s!

Lady Wilde was very disappointed with Oscar when he was born. She wanted a girl, not another boy. She compensated by dressing the poor child in all the frills and flounces she would have lavished on a girl, encouraged his hair to grow into long curls and turned them into ringlets. Oscar wrote in *The Importance of Being Ernest*, 'All women become like their mothers. That is their tragedy. No man does. That's his.' He was about 9 years of age before he was allowed to dress as a boy. She would probably have dressed him as a girl for longer if he hadn't grown so broad and tall. He was over 6ft when he was aged 17. Another reason for dressing him as a boy was the necessity of giving him a good education. He was sent, as a boarder, to Portora Royal, a school for boys in Enniskillen in County Fermanagh.

Portora Royal was founded along with Armagh Royal and Dungannon Royal by King James I in 1608. It was one of the oldest schools in Ireland. It was amalgamated with Enniskillen Collegiate Grammar School on 1 September 2016 and renamed Enniskillen Royal Grammar School. One of Oscar's teachers, J.F. Davies, published an edition of *Agamemnon of Aeschylus*, a story about a Greek king going to war (the Trojan War), winning the war and coming home, where he was murdered. Young Oscar was so intrigued he learned reams of the play and kept quoting from it! He was an excellent scholar who won a scholarship to attend Trinity College, Dublin (1871–74). The school was very proud of its scholarship winners and inscribed his name on one of the school's blackboards. In 1895, when he fell into disgrace and was sent to jail for being homosexual, which seems almost unbelievable today, his name was painted out. He had carved his initials on a window of a classroom and the then headmaster patiently scraped them out! In more enlightened times his name was re-gilded on the school's roll of honour.

The English department in Portora Royal School was amazing. As well as nurturing Oscar Wilde it also nurtured the talent of Samuel Beckett, playwright, novelist and poet, who won a Nobel Prize for English Literature (1969) and whose work included the play *Waiting for Godot*.

Oscar had been christened Oscar Fingal O'Flahertie Wills Wilde. He must have felt he was destined for greatness because he said:

> My name has two Os, two Fs and two Ws. A name which is too long to be in everyone's mouth. It comes so expensive in the advertisement. When one is unknown, a number of Christian names are useful. As one becomes famous, one sheds some of them, just as a balloonist, when rising higher, sheds unnecessary ballast … all but two of my unnecessary names have already been thrown overboard. Soon I shall discard another and be known simply as 'The Wild' or simply 'The Oscar'.

When Wilde left Dublin he moved to Magdalen Oxford (1874–78) and began to create the legend of Oscar by becoming 'Professor of Aesthetics'. He designed his own clothes, consisting of a loose shirt with a turn-down collar and a huge tie, which was usually green and tied in a very big knot. He loved flowers and always had one in his buttonhole. He particularly loved big flowers such as sunflowers, lilies and poppies. Of course, people made fun of him. The then editor of *Punch* wrote a play called *The Colonel* ridiculing him, and a caricature of his personality was featured in Gilbert and Sullivan's operetta *Patience*. Many people hoped that poking fun at him would cause his downfall. It did no such thing. It made him famous and he was sent on a lecture tour, on aestheticism, to America to advertise the production of *Patience* and make sure it was a success.

Oscar arrived in New York saying, 'I have nothing to declare but my genius.' He talked to all kinds of people, including miners, cowboys and screaming hordes of women. He said that while in America he had to hire two secretaries, one with brown hair, who was becoming rapidly bald as his job was to send locks of his own hair to ladies who wrote asking for Oscar's, and the other to 'write my autograph and answer the hundreds of letters that come begging for it'! Although he lectured in his aesthetic attire, he didn't carry either a sunflower or a poppy in America. He changed his image, becoming more of a man of the Wild West with the knee boots, ten-gallon hat and kerchief of the cowboy. He said:

> The crude commercialism of America, its materialist spirit, its indifference to the poetical side of things, and its lack of imagination and of high unattainable ideals, are entirely due to that country having adopted for its national hero a man, who according to his own confession, was incapable of telling a lie, and it is not too much to say that the story of George Washington and the cherry-tree has done more harm in a shorter period of time than any other moral tale in the whole of literature – and the amusing part of the whole thing is that the story of the cherry-tree is an absolute myth.

Oscar was a riot wherever he went, and more popular than ever when he came back to England. The American tour made Oscar! He described the world's troubles in a unique way, assuring his listeners that most people die of 'creeping common sense'. He didn't suffer fools gladly but had an uncanny ability to make

'Yer man says he's nothin' til declare apart from his genius!'

sensible men appear foolish. For instance, once when he was a guest of Frank Harris, who began talking about all the famous houses in London where he had dined, Oscar became bored and said, 'Yes my dear Frank, we believe you've dined in every house in London, once.'

In 1881 Oscar is listed as a boarder in 1 (now 44) Tite Street, Chelsea. Frank Miles, a society painter, was head of the household and it was here that Oscar met Lillie Langtry, said to be 'the most glamorous woman in England'. They became great friends. He once said, 'I would rather have discovered Lillie Langtry than to have discovered America.' He taught her Latin and encouraged her to pursue an acting career. In her autobiography she wrote he 'possesses a remarkably fascinating and compelling personality'.

In 1881 he was introduced to Constance Loyd, who was the daughter of Horace Lloyd. She visited Dublin in 1884 when Oscar was lecturing at the Gaiety Theatre and he proposed to her. They married at St James Anglican Church in Paddington, and renovated their home, 16 Tite Street, so it reflected their luxurious aesthetic taste. They had two sons: Cyril, who was born in 1885, and Vyvyan, who followed in 1886.

Oscar became the editor of *The Lady's World Magazine* in 1887. He changed its name to *The Woman's World*. He kept the discussions of fashion and arts but added serious articles on all sorts of things like politics, culture and parenting along with two stories, one for the ladies and one to be read to children. He wrote 'Literary and Other Notes', which were amusing and very popular. He wrote nine plays between the years 1879 and 1894, including *The Importance of Being Ernest*, *A Woman of No Importance*, *Lady Windermere's Fan* and *An Ideal Husband*. They have stood the test of time and are still enjoyed today, as is his only novel, *The Picture of Dorian Gray*. It's a story of a beautiful young man who has his portrait painted and sells his soul to the Devil so he will remain beautiful no matter how badly he behaves. He puts the painting in the attic and all the evil things he does in his life are recorded on the painting while his face remains beautiful. Eventually the face on the painting looks so awful and Dorian is so horrified he takes a knife and stabs it. His servants hear a scream, rush up to the attic and find a very evil-looking old man lying dead on the floor with a knife in his chest with the picture of a beautiful young man hanging above him. In his novel Oscar wrote, 'Modern morality consists in accepting the standard of one's age. I consider that for any man of culture to accept the standard of his age is the grossest immorality.'

Although he was married and had sired two children, Oscar was homosexual. He became a lover of Lord Alfred Bruce Douglas (1870–1945), known as Bosie Douglas, an English poet and journalist. Homosexuality was illegal until 1960. Oscar foolishly took Bosie's father, Lord Douglas, the 9th Marquess of Queensbury (1844–1900), to court for libel because he'd left a calling card to Oscar addressed to a 'posing sodomite'. Unfortunately during the court proceedings Oscar was found guilty of being a homosexual and sent to gaol for two years. That's where he wrote the poem 'The Ballad of Reading Gaol', which describes how he felt in prison and his sympathy for a man who was sentenced to death.

Some verses:

He walked amongst the Trial Men
In a suit of shabby grey;
A cricket cap was on his head,
And his step seemed light and gay;
But I never saw a man who looked
So wistfully at the day.

I walked, with other souls in pain,
Within another ring,
And was wondering if the man had done
A great or little thing,
When a voice behind me whispered low,
'That fellow's got to swing.'

I only knew what hunted thought
Quickened his step, and why
He looked upon the garish day
With such a wistful eye;
The man had killed the thing he loved,
And so he had to die.

Oscar Wilde

Constance was devastated by Oscar's homosexuality, trial and gaol sentence. They killed his marriage. Apart from the feelings a wife would feel today, she had to cope with the shame caused by the attitudes of Victorian society. She divorced him, got custody of their sons, changed her name, and those of their sons, to Holland, and moved to Switzerland, where she enrolled them in an English-speaking school. Oscar must have found that heart-breaking because he was an excellent father. He loved his children, spent a lot of time with them, told them stories and wrote stories for children.

When he got out of gaol Oscar and Bosie travelled in Europe for a few years, then they fell out and separated. Oscar moved to Paris and died in penury. He remained an aesthetic to the last. He hated the ugly wallpaper in the room where his life ended. His last words were, 'One of us has to go!'

Northern Ireland is a very small area (about the same size as Yorkshire) with an amazing number of other writers associated with it, including three Nobel Prizes for English Literature, namely W.B. Yeats (1923), Samuel Beckett (1969) and Seamus Heaney (1995). There was also Jonathan Swift, the Brontës and C.S. Lewis, among others.

W.B. Yeats (1865–1939) had a close connection with County Down. His grandfather was the rector of Tullylish Anglican Church. He won the Nobel Prize for English Literature in 1923. (See Yeats Family.)

Samuel Beckett (1906–89) was of Huguenot stock. His father, William Frank Beckett, was a quantity surveyor. His mother, Maria Jones Roe, was a nurse. He received his early education around the area in which he had been born; then, like Oscar Wilde, attended Portora Royal School in Enniskillen, County Fermanagh, starting around 1919–20. He left in 1923 and went on to obtain his degree in 1927 from Trinity College, Dublin, and spent most of his adult life living in France writing in both English and French. His most famous play, *Waiting for Godot* (1953), was written in French, then translated into English. He also wrote *Endgame* and *Happy Times*. He was a poet, novelist, dramatist, short story writer, theatre director and literary translator. As his career progressed, he became more and more minimalist. He is famous, among other things, for the following sayings: 'We are all born mad. Some remain so,' 'Words are all we have', and 'Every word is like an unnecessary stain on silence and nothingness'.

Beckett was a natural athlete who played cricket as a left-handed batsman and a left-arm medium bowler. He played for Dublin University and played two first-class games against Northamptonshire. He's the only Nobel literature laureate to have played first-class cricket and appear in *Wisden*, the bible of cricket history!

Seamus Heaney (1939–2013) was born on his family farm, Mossbawn, near Castledawson in County Londonderry, was educated in St Columba's College in Derry and obtained his degree through Queen's University, Belfast. Seamus described his childhood as 'an intimate, physical, creaturely existence … in suspension between the archaic and the modern' and its influence can be seen clearly in his poetry.

In the 1990s, when the John Hewitt Summer School was based in Garron Tower, a boys' boarding school on the Antrim Coast, I was privileged to meet Seamus's younger brother, the late Hugh Heaney. He had a wicked sense of humour and I was told that he boasted he wrote better poetry than Seamus and had been interviewed by a reporter from the *Daily Mail*. I asked Hugh about his poetry and the interview. He laughed and said:

> Yes! I was ploughing a field when I noticed this fella obviously wanting to talk to me. He waved me down so I invited him up into the tractor and continued ploughing. When he asked about my poetry I told him it is definitely much better than Seamus's. Then he asked what I've published. I pretended to be annoyed! 'It's all in my head!' I said 'I've the family farm to run. I don't have the luxury of enough time to write my poetry down. I've got to get on with making a living.'

Hugh was very proud of his famous brother. He said, 'I laugh and joke, but I think what Seamus has achieved is great. When he's at home he's just another brother. His feet have never left the ground. In a way he's never left Bellaghy.' I can back that up from personal experience. I was acquainted with both Seamus Heaney and his wife Marie. I found them very down to earth, friendly, pleasant people. They never got what is described in Northern Ireland as 'up themselves'! I remember chatting to him after a performance of his play *The Cure at Troy* in the Lyric Theatre, Belfast. I said, 'Seamus, that play must be really good because I'm Philistine and I was dragged out tonight by my husband. I didn't want to come. I was tired and wanted to doze at home, yet I sat entranced by your words.' Seamus smiled and said, 'It helps that somebody else wrote it first!'

Hugh was in his late 70s when he died in September 2021. Seamus died in 2013, but before he died he wrote a touching tribute to Hugh in the form of a poem titled 'Keeping Going'.

Jonathan Swift's (1667–1745) most famous works are *Gulliver's Travels* (1726), *A Modest Proposal* (1729) and *A Tale of a Tub* (1704). He was educated at Kilkenny School and Trinity College Dublin, and qualified as an Anglican member of the cloth, his first parish being Kilroot, near Carrickfergus in County Antrim. He hated it, in fact he disliked the whole of Ireland intensely. Local tradition says in Kilroot he lived in a house without any corners so the Devil couldn't hide in them. The church at Kilroot has long gone but it was once connected with Ballynure Anglican Church, which bears a plaque remembering he preached there. My old friend and local historian, the late Ernie Scott, was a native of Ballynure. He told me the congregation of Ballynure did not appreciate him. They didn't go to church if Jonathan was preaching because his sermons were so long. One Sunday, Swift decided to do something about his lack of a congregation. He started gathering rocks and carrying them inside the church. The news spread quickly around the village and people wondered what he was up to. They came to watch, became more curious and eventually began to go into the church. When he reckoned he had a large enough number inside he locked all the doors and preached for eight hours! The good people of Ballynure never forgave him!

Swift had troubled relationships with two women, Esther Johnston (Stella) and Esther Vanhomrigh (Vanessa). Eventually he became Dean of St Patrick's Cathedral, Dublin. He is buried beside Stella in St Patrick's. He wrote his own epitaph:

Verses on the Death of Dr Dean Swift
My female friends, whose tender hearts
Have better earned to act their parts,
Receive the news in doleful dumps,
The Dean is dead, (and what is trumps?)

Patrick Brontë (1777–1861) had a profound influence on his famous daughters, Charlotte, Emily and Anne. He was born at Emdale, a two-bedroom cottage in the townland of Dumballyroney, County Down. He was the eldest son of Hugh Bronte and Elinor Alice (née McCrory) Bronte. The daughters' story ends in Haworth in Yorkshire, but it began in County Down. Their father, Revd Patrick Brontë, was born of humble farming stock. Over time the family name changed from Prunty to Bronte and eventually to Brontë. Pruntys and Brontes still exist around the area.

Patrick's parents, Hugh Brunty and Alice McCrory, were married in Magerally Church in 1776. The officiating clergyman said Alice was the most beautiful bride he had ever seen. The young couple began their married life by living with Alice's brother until they found a two-bedroom cottage nearby. They used one room as a bedroom and parlour, the other as a corn kiln, kitchen and reception room.

Patrick was born on St Patrick's Day 1777 and was Christened in Drumgooland Parish Church, Ballyward. He was the eldest of ten children and the family could be described as very poor, but respectable. They owned four books, two of which were the Bible, and the children were fed on buttermilk, potatoes and bread, which Patrick insisted caused him to have stomach problems throughout his life! They aimed to be self-sufficient. Alice got wool from her brother's sheep and spun it into thread, and as a result Patrick refused to wear garments made of anything other than wool. He said if he was dressed in cotton he'd catch his death of cold! His first job as a weaver enabled him to make sure his family were self-sufficient regarding clothing. Although they were poor, they were literate and believed in education for all, a viewpoint Patrick inherited. He made sure his daughters were well educated, which was an unusual attitude at the time. There was a glen opposite the family home, which for the younger generation was the equivalent of the street corner or teenager's den. Fiddle playing, dancing, games and songs. This was the environment for the young Patrick: hard-grafting, poor parents, the product of a mixed marriage in a country driven by power struggles defined in religious terms. His family were not part of the mainstream; they were free thinkers and so was he. His father, Hugh Brunty, was a gifted storyteller who held his family and neighbours enthralled. Patrick inherited his father's gift and passed it on to his children.

Patrick's first job was as a weaver. He found weaving boring so he used to work with a book propped up on the loom in front of him. As a result he made mistakes and got the sack. His County Down upbringing was evident throughout his life. Having been sacked as a weaver, Patrick got a job teaching in Glascar School. Unfortunately he fell in love with one of his pupils and although there was very little difference in their ages he was sacked! Then he was very lucky as he got a post at Drumballyroney School. He was taken under the wing of the rector, the Revd Thomas Tighe, who encouraged him to apply for a university education. He won a scholarship to attend St John's College, Cambridge. He obtained his degree and was ordained as a clergyman. When Patrick went to Cambridge, he must have felt very strange, a rough country lad in the middle of well-educated academics. That is where the change of name occurred. There are two theories regarding the acquisition of the 'ë'. Possibly the registrar made a mistake when Patrick was registering in Cambridge, or Patrick realised the similarity of his name to the Brontë region in Sicily on the northern slopes of Mount Etna. Lord Nelson, in recognition of his services during the Napoleonic Wars, had been awarded the Duchy of Brontë in Sicily by King Ferdinand III of Italy. Patrick was an admirer of Lord Nelson, so may have made the minor adjustment to his name.

Patrick Brontë preached his first sermon in Drumballyroney Church, which has since been decommissioned. The churchyard contains a Brontë grave. If you want to visit it, go behind the church keeping close to the church.

C.S. Lewis (1898–1963) is well known as an Anglican theologian, an academic (he was employed as a lecturer at both Oxford and Cambridge Universities), and the author of many books on theology, poetry and the series of children's books known collectively as *The Chronicles of Narnia*. They have become classics and became more successful since his death in 1963, with *The Lion, the Witch and the Wardrobe* having been turned into a West End musical and a movie. What

Aslan, as depicted in the Narnia Trail in Kilbroney Forest Park.

CS Lewis Square, Holywood Arches, Belfast.

is less well known is that Clive Staples Lewis was born and bred in Belfast and was proud of the city with its rich maritime and industrial history. He was the younger son of Albert and Flora. At the time of his birth, Belfast was one of the most thriving cities in Western Europe. It could claim the greatest shipyard, rope works, tobacco factory, linen mill, dry dock and tea machinery works in the world. It had the largest gantry in the British Isles and had launched *Oceanic*, which was then the biggest ship afloat. The imaginations of Clive and his elder brother, Warren, were inspired by a telescope in their bedroom from which they could see the shipyard, the hills of County Antrim, Belfast Lough and the night sky.

One of the highlights of Lewis family life was when their mother took the brothers on their annual holiday, which was usually in Castlerock. They usually spent about six weeks there. Clive learned to swim and to love the Irish landscape during visits to nearby resorts of Portrush, Downhill and Ballycastle. It gave him an endless source of inspiration and a link with his past. As an adult he retained the ability to look at the world through the eyes, and imagination, of a child. That's what makes his stories so vivid.

He told his brother, Warren, that the idea for Narnia came from the County Down area in the shadow of the Mourne Mountains overlooking Carlingford Lough, which is part of Kilbroney Park. It now contains a place called Narnia with sculptures of characters in the books. He is also remembered in CS Lewis Square near the Holywood Arches in East Belfast.

P

PADDY ALI

Paddy Monaghan (1944–2017) became known as Paddy Ali. He was a World Champion Bare Knuckle Boxer, who was born, and reared, in Ederney, County Fermanagh, and became a close friend of Muhammad Ali. Their friendship began after Paddy Ali had moved to England to find work. He was living in Saxton Road, one of the worst streets in Abingdon, near Oxford.

Paddy Ali was an admirer of the World Heavyweight Champion Cassius Clay, who is rated as one of the greatest boxing champions of all time. He boasted he could 'float like a butterfly, sting like a bee'. He was born into a Baptist family and experienced a lot of discrimination because of his colour, so when he was a teenager he became interested in the Muslim faith, eventually becoming a Muslim. He kept his change of faith a secret at first in case it hindered his boxing career.

Cassius Clay won a gold medal in the 1960 Olympic Games and was recognised as a hero. When he returned home to America he was turned away from a restaurant because of his colour. He was enraged, threw his gold medal into the Ohio River and changed his name to Muhammad Ali. He took his new religion, with its message of love and peace, very seriously and refused to fight in the Vietnam War. As a result, the American government stripped him of the world heavyweight title he'd won in 1967. Back in England, Paddy Ali was furious. He thought the American government's actions were outrageous and described Ali as 'the people's champion'. He organised a petition that eventually contained 22,024 signatures, a tremendous feat in the days before computers. He was so angry that he wrote to President Nixon to object.

Ali was very grateful and went to visit Paddy at his tiny terrace house in Paxton Road, Abingdon. His presence caused mayhem! So many people came to see him the police couldn't cope and the army had to be called in.

Ali had tea with the Monaghans, entertained the local children by doing card tricks and sparred with the local boys, including Paddy's 16-year-old son. The two men struck up a close friendship and Ali invited Paddy to visit him at his home in America. The two men got on so well that Ali invited Paddy's family to come and live near him. However, Paddy turned down what was a very generous offer because he loved his homeland. When he retired he returned to County Fermanagh, where he died in April 2021, aged 73.

POITEEN

Poiteen, also known as Mountain Dew, is illegal whiskey made surreptitiously, hidden well away from revenue men! It was criminalised in 1661 and driven underground, where it stays!

As far as I can ascertain, Fermanagh is the 'capital' of poiteen making. It's not as closely scrutinised as the counties near the east coast of Northern Ireland, so people are less likely to be caught. The late Paddy Cassidy said:

> There're so many islands in Fermanagh's lakes, the likelihood of the revenue men guessing where you are is remote. If by chance somebody does guess, you've a handy place to throw the evidence. I know a man who was making poiteen on his farm. His lookouts warned him the revenue men were coming so he threw it in to his duck pond. His ducks drank the pond water and became drunk. As yer man said, 'It was quare good stuff and a terrible pity til waste it.' He found watching his drunken ducks staggering around embarrassing and told the revenue men he thought they were suffering from vertigo!
>
> A lot of people have learned how to row backwards so they look as if they're coming towards you and they're actually going away! The disadvantage of an island is it can be cold. People have been known to die of hypothermia while watching a still, but you're all right if you lie on a bed of stones. With any luck they aren't wet and they retain heat. You're landed if you have two dogs. Put one at your head and one at your feet. Dogs make great hot-water bottles!

Pat also told me that Fermanagh's bogs are great places to make poiteen. I asked if that wasn't dangerous because you could get trapped in a bog, sink under the surface and die.

He said:

> You could, but don't forget locals know the countryside like the back of their hands. They know where it's safe. Bogs can be dangerous, that's why they're so good for making poiteen. The revenue men don't know where to look for it and are scared to go off the beaten paths looking. If you're making poiteen in a bog you need a horse as well as a dog.

Lough Erne, Fermanagh's Lakeland.

I asked, 'Why do you need a horse?' Pat replied:

> Well! It's like this. You could become a trifle befuddled tasting the poiteen as it comes out of the still. Ye have to make sure it's alcohol coming out, not water. A mist could come down and what with you being befuddled and not being able to see you could end up in the bog. A horse always knows its way home. If you're in such a bad way you can't get on the horse, all you do is hold on to its tail and walk behind it.
>
> Poiteen is usually made by fermenting potatoes. Some people use beetroot and most people have their own favourite recipe. The brew starts of as a wine which needs to be distilled by being boiled and passed through a condenser. Alcohol evaporates before water so you must test the taste every now and again to make sure it's alcohol you're collecting. Mind you, you don't want to drink pure alcohol. It's poisonous, so it is! Making poiteen's a very simple process. If you spot revenue men coming it's possible to break your apparatus up and runners can take different bits of it in different directions so them revenue spoilsports can only suspect the worst. They can't prove it. Yes! I know poiteen making's illegal, but it's poor farming country out here and you have to live!

Men weren't the only ones to make poiteen, women also became expert. Ann Murray lived in Glenariff in the nineteenth century and supported herself by knitting and sewing and distilling her own poiteen. She got round the liquor laws by selling water to customers and giving them free poiteen! She lived in a cave in Red Bay and was popular with locals and travellers seeking refreshment to speed them on their journey. Ann only faced the law twice and was sentenced to the county jail. She was lucky because avoiding excise duty would have been considered a fairly major crime at the time. People found guilty of committing 'minor crimes', such a stealing a loaf of bread, could be transported to Australia. It is thought that Lord Antrim used his influence to enable her to continue with her work. She didn't pay rent, or for a licence, because he was told exhausted travellers found it very difficult to travel along the coast and they benefited from her business. In 1847 the *Belfast Vindicator* newspaper wrote that 'few tourists to the causeway have passed by these caves without paying a passing visit to Nanny', as she was known to locals. She lived to be over 100 years of age!

The majority of the population in Ireland lived at subsistence levels during the eighteenth and early nineteenth century. Living in caves, or holes in the ground that were roughly thatched, was not uncommon. Such poverty-stricken people had no legal means of support and making poiteen provided a means of making a little money. Ann Murray was not the only cave-dwelling poiteen producer. For instance, Belfast's Cave Hill has three caves, one of which was also a shebeen (a place where it was possible to buy alcohol illegally).

Q

QUEEN OF LONDON COURTESANS

Laura Bell, Queen of London Courtesans, was born in Dublin about 1829, the daughter of Robert Henry Bell and Laura Jane Seymour. Her mother was the illegitimate daughter of the 3rd Marquess of Hertford and her father was the bailiff for the 4th Marquess. She grew up at Bellbrook House, Glenavy, County Antrim. (The word 'courtesan' may not be understood in Northern Ireland. 'Prostitute' yes or possibly 'whore', pronounced 'Who-eer', not to be confused with a 'cute who-eer', which in the south of Ireland means a politician.)

Laura left home when she was 14 and went to work in a draper's shop in Belfast. She had an attractive, vivacious personality and was very pretty, with a small doll-like face, blonde curly hair, a peaches and cream complexion and beautiful, big blue eyes. She used her attributes to begin a lucrative career as a prostitute. She was very successful in her new career but realised she could make more money in Dublin, so moved there. She wanted to be an actress but did not succeed in that ambition. However, her vivacious character and stunning beauty enabled her to be a great success as a courtesan. Oscar Wilde's father, Dr William Wilde, a well-respected society dentist, was one of her clients.

Sometime around 1849, when Ireland was suffering terribly from the effects of the Great Famine, and having accumulated gifts and money from her lovers, Laura left for London. She found employment in Jay's General Mourning House in Regent Street, which sold everything to do with death – coffins, mourning rings and so on – before resuming her career as a courtesan. She was a great success, entertained rich noblemen and earned the title of 'Queen of London Whoredom'. She often drove in a gilt carriage, drawn by two white horses, around Hyde Park, where she met the Nepalese Prime Minister, Jung Bahadur Rana. He showered her with presents and gave her a luxury house in Wilton Crescent, Belgravia. (It was said that he paid £250,000 for one night with her, but it's more likely that was the total value of gifts given to her during the ninety days they spent together.) Her lover was heartbroken when he had to go back to

Nepal. He gave her a priceless diamond ring and promised that in the future he'd help her in any way he could. He kept his promise, because Laura wrote to him during the Indian Mutiny when she heard of the plight of besieged British officers and their families at Lucknow and asked him to send troops to help the British. She enclosed the ring to remind him of his promise. He couldn't say 'no!' to her and led his own troops to help the British break the siege.

Laura married Captain Augustus Frederick Thistlethwayte on 19 October 1852 and her life changed forever because marriage gave her a veneer of respectability. He was very wealthy, with a house in Grosvenor Square and an estate in Scotland. Laura's extravagance caused trouble in her marriage, so the couple usually didn't live together. In 1856, Laura heard Richard Weaver preach. He had been a prize fighter and a hard drinker who had converted to Christianity. He was so eloquent both Laura and her husband experienced a religious conversion and Laura became a revivalist preacher on morality! She referred to herself as 'God's Ambassadress'. She gained a following because of her attractive personality and her eloquent sermons were mesmerising. A visitor to one of her services in 1865 published his thoughts in the *Cork Constitution* of 11 April 1865, stating:

> Precisely at three o'clock a side door on the platform was opened, and I at once recognised Mrs Thistlethwayte. She looks in the very prime of womanhood. Her beautiful light brown hair was worn perfectly plain, and on her head she had a little black bonnet, well thrown back with ruche inside, and long strings of tulle hanging down. She wore a dress of thick black silk, with embroidered epaulets and cuffs; plain white linen collar, and under sleeves, the latter fastened with colitaires. Advancing at once to the table, she said, 'Let us sing the 60th hymn in the book.' … Mrs Thistlethwayte reads beautifully. She has a soft, yet powerful, and admirably modulated voice; but she opens her mouth to a greater extent more than is necessary, probably with a desire to give as much volume as possible to her voice … She next offered up a prayer, after which another hymn was sung. The text of the sermon was the 21st verse of the 10th of Luke. Upon this subject she enlarged for nearly an hour, with a propriety of expression, an eloquence of diction, and rapidity of elocution, positively amazing. The manner of delivery was, perhaps, a little jerky here and there, and she occasionally clenched her hand unnecessarily but as a whole, the effect was most impressive, and I don't think anyone who heard her went away unimproved. At the conclusion she offered up another prayer, and then withdrew, accompanied by some half-dozen of the pragmatic ladies in rich garments.

Laura's husband accidentally shot himself in 1887. Every morning he used to summon his valet by firing into the ceiling of his bedroom with a pistol he kept in his bedside table. It's thought that he staggered, fell and accidentally shot himself. He died fourteen hours later. Laura never married again. She continued hosting evangelical tea parties for high society, became a friend of the Prime Minister, William Ewart Gladstone, and his wife, and helped London's prostitutes by giving the money she earned preaching the gospel to them. In spite of her religious conversion, she was never cured of her lavish spending habits and spent her life being chased by debt collectors. She eventually sold her house in Belgravia and went to live in Woodbine Cottage in West Hampstead. It had belonged to her husband. She died quietly there in 1894 after an amazing life that started with a childhood spent in what locals would call 'a wee small village' in County Antrim.

R

RUPERTS

Rupert was a British Army name given by those without a commission; in other words, it's what the 'other ranks' called their officers, who they disliked. They considered them too posh for their own good and that they were 'wet behind their ears'. During the Second World War, between 1943 and 1944, dummies made from cloth and called 'Rupert' were made secretly by women in a factory in Carrickfergus, which was then a small town in County Antrim, about 10 miles north-east of Belfast. Their function was to look like paratroopers. They were part of Operation Titanic, a distraction excercise on D-Day, 6 June 1944. Ruperts were attached to a miniature parachute and had small explosives tied on them. Planes dropped them above forests in France a few miles inland from the beaches in Normandy, where the Allied forces intended to invade. Thousands of Ruperts were dropped and exploded so they sounded like a large air invasion.

My friend Adrian Hack told me that when his mother-in-law was a young woman, she assembled parachutes in the Carrickfergus factory, which became the largest such facility in the world. In the early years of the war, the government commissioned reports on the viability of converting existing manufacturing businesses into ones that could support the needs of the military. Barn Mills, the factory in question, was identified as one that could be repurposed. In 1942 the Littlewoods Company, based in the north of England, took over the company and began work on repurposing the building. They retrained the existing workforce and recruited new machinists. At the time it was on the outskirts of the town. It had been built in the 1790s as a cotton mill, then in the middle of the nineteenth century it adapted to be part of the burgeoning linen industry developing within Northern Ireland. The town of Carrickfergus had a population of just 4,500 at the start of the Second World War, so the factory relied on women from the surrounding area to come to Carrickfergus and work there. Within twelve months, more than 1,000 people, mainly women, were working in the factory, initially producing parachutes. It took six women to make each parachute: one to cut the material (silk, and later a silk/polyester mix) from a pattern; an assembler, who loosely stitched the component parts together; a stitcher who put double seams down each join; harnesses and cables were attached; a packer folded the parachute in a specific manner and put it into the 'chute pack'; and finally a supervisor ensured quality control. Each group of six women was expected to create a minimum of four parachutes per day, with the more experienced ones able to produce six or seven. When the necessary skills and logistics developed, the factory took on other projects. A small number of large helium balloons, used as target practice by anti-aircraft crews, were made, followed by a significant number of Mae West life jackets.

From late 1943 to mid-1944, some of the factory girls worked, in secret, to make Ruperts. The Germans identified these as a large paratrooper assault, just as intended. On contact with the ground, the small explosives went off, not to cause harm but to sound like grenades. There is no doubt that the hard work of the women back in Barn Mills helped save hundreds of lives on D-Day because the enemy diverted troops to deal with the perceived invasion of paratroopers.

Other factories were repurposed to build tanks, assemble uniforms, supply webbing used as belts and straps by the army, and one became a military prison.

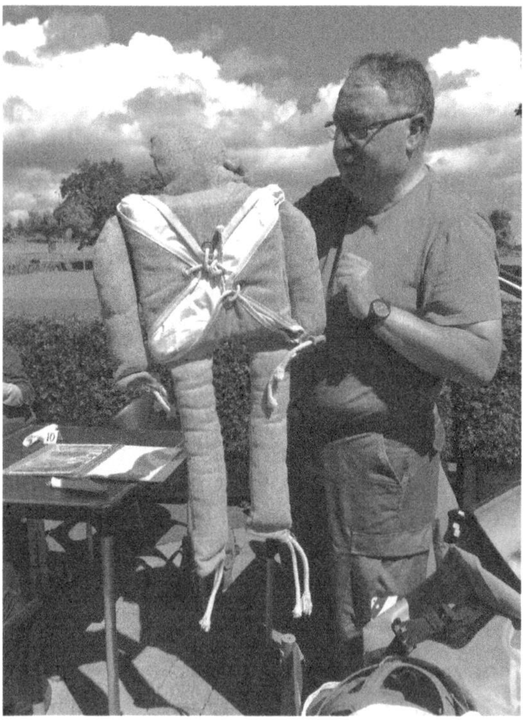

A Rupert held by Adrian Hack (Photograph printed by kind permission of Adrian Hack)

S

ST PATRICK

St Patrick is the Patron Saint of the whole of Ireland, although he spent most of his time in the north. We know a lot about him because two letters written by him have survived, namely his 'Confession' and his 'Letter to Coroticus'.

In his 'Confession', St Patrick says he was the son of a wealthy Roman Christian family, who lived in Britain at a place called Bannavem Taburniae. Unfortunately nobody is entirely certain where that was! Recent archaeological finds make it likely to have been a small settlement, called Banna, near Birdoswald Roman Fort, on Hadrian's Wall, 15 miles from Carlisle (Luguvalium).

St Patrick's grandfather was a devout Christian. His father, Calpurnius, was a deacon in the Church and a politician. It's impossible to tell if his beliefs were those of a sincere Christian or if they were motivated by politics. In those days it was a 'posh' thing to be a Christian and an active member of the Church. It helped in business dealings.

When St Patrick was 15 years of age his parents were away from home and his house was raided by a bunch of pirates, who captured people and sold them as slaves. They killed the old and infirm as there wasn't any point in allowing anyone who couldn't do a hard day's work to live. They'd just eat food, be difficult to sell and not be an economic proposition. They kidnapped those who looked strong enough to make valuable slaves. The young Patrick and his sister, Lupita, appeared strong and healthy so they survived. Patrick was sold to a man called Milchiu, who lived on Slemish Mountain, while Lupita was sold as a hand maiden to a family who lived in County Louth.

According to the book *Ten Thousand Saints: A Study in Irish and European Origins* by Hubert Butler, Lupita also became a saint, although she was found in the bed of her nephew, St Mel. He was at confession and she said she'd climbed into his bed to gain sanity from the sheets! She got away with that and moved to Armagh, where she acted as a prostitute. Eventually she annoyed St Patrick by sleeping with St Colman, a saint he didn't like. St Patrick was so enraged he took his chariot and killed her by running it three times over her body. He held confession for her as her soul entered heaven. That's a strange tale when viewed through today's eyes. It was probably invented to enhance St Patrick's reputation but it maligns him. There's no evidence he ever had a horse, never mind a chariot. He travelled on foot.

Patrick was a nominal Christian until he hit 'the road to Damascus' on a freezing cold, wet day on Slemish Mountain. He couldn't find all his sheep and was terrified! He knew slaves were beaten severely when they lost animals. He fell to his knees and prayed as he'd never prayed before. He told God how frightened he felt, how he was miserable in this strange land and how he hated being a slave. His prayer resulted in a tremendous feeling of peace. He found his animals and stayed out of trouble. After that he often went out in freezing weather to pray. He felt very close to Jesus in that type of condition. At first the other slaves thought he was stark staring raving mad, but gradually his belief and behaviour impressed them and many of them converted to Christianity.

After six years of slavery, Patrick heard God telling him to escape. He must have felt he was going crazy because in those days slaves didn't dare escape! It was too risky. There was nowhere to go as Ireland's a small country. Communities were small and everyone knew everyone else. Strangers were unwelcome. Slaves were easily identified because they were dressed differently from the general population. A runaway slave would have stuck out like a sore thumb. Escaped slaves were returned to their owners and tortured to death as a warning to the others.

Eventually Patrick became convinced God really did want him to escape, as His voice kept saying, 'Do not be afraid. I will be with you every step of the way.'

Patrick wrote that he walked 200 miles to the coast. Slemish Mountain is only a few miles from County Antrim's coast, so Patrick must have walked inland. Croagh Patrick in County Mayo is about 200 miles from Slemish, so perhaps that explains the close connection between St Patrick and County Mayo? He kept out of sight by travelling during the hours of darkness and fed off the land. Eventually he came to the sea and hid in a shepherd's hut until God told him his ship was ready. He looked out and saw a ship in the harbour so he went and asked the captain for a job. He must have been very disappointed when the captain said, 'No way!' He turned on his heel and began to walk away but the captain had a change of heart and shouted after him, 'Could you look after our dogs?' Patrick said he could and was told to come on board.

The ship set sail and a terrible storm blew up. Patrick and the sailors were shipwrecked on a barren, uninhabited land. They walked and walked until they could go no further and some of the sailors began to fall by the wayside. The captain flew into a rage and was going to murder Patrick. He yelled at the poor man, 'I shouldn't have allowed you to come on board! You've brought a curse on us. We've been shipwrecked and are going to die of starvation!' St Patrick fell to his knees and prayed for food and a herd of pigs appeared! The sailors caught, killed and cooked them. Everybody had enough to eat, St Patrick's life was saved and the sailors were able to go back and rescue their companions who'd fallen by the wayside.

Nobody knows where St Patrick went after the shipwreck. All that is known is that he trained as a clergyman and eventually managed to return home to Banavem Taburniae, where he was reunited with his parents. They must have been astonished to see him. Slaves never escaped, never mind made it back home!

St Patrick wrote in his 'Confession' that he was 'a miserable sinner' who was uneducated and who had committed a 'terrible sin' in his youth. He was haunted with guilt. Eventually his best friend persuaded him to confess, to get it off his chest, so to speak, and to forget about it. St Patrick trusted his friend and wept as he narrated what he'd done. He found confessing a relief. Later when he believed God wanted him go back to Ireland and tell the inhabitants about Jesus, becoming a bishop was a necessary qualification. When he applied to be consecrated his friend proved false, broke his promise and told the Church hierarchy about Patrick's 'terrible sin'. As a result, it was decided that Patrick was not a suitable candidate. Patrick was very persistent so he sat down and wrote his 'Confession' to persuade them they should grant his wish. He said he was motivated by a strong desire to tell the Irish about the love of God and described himself in the following words quoted from his 'Confession': 'I, Patrick, a sinner, a most simple countryman, the least of all the faithful and most contemptible to many …'

He explained his motivation by writing:

> In a vision of the night I saw a man whose name was Victorious coming as if from Ireland with innumerable letters … and they were crying as if with one voice: 'We beg you, holy youth, that you shall come and walk again among us.' And I was stung intensely in my heart …

He was very persistent, so the Church hierarchy probably got fed up saying 'no' and granted his wish. It's likely they thought him working as a missionary in Ireland would solve their problem because he'd be murdered. At that time, Ireland was a very dangerous place. Its inhabitants had a nasty habit of killing strangers on sight and stealing their possessions.

St Patrick began his missionary work in County Down. He and some of his followers landed where the River Slaney runs into Strangford Lough, near where the village of Strangford is situated today. They hid their boat, began walking inland and were spotted by a local shepherd boy. He told his master, a chieftain called Dichu, who had a huge dog, probably an Irish wolfhound, that was trained to kill strangers on sight. Dichu walked towards St Patrick and released his hound, fully expecting the saint to be torn to shreds. The animal charged towards the saint, licked his hand and lay meekly down at his feet. Dichu was astonished. St Patrick said, 'Jesus looks after me. Nothing can hurt me. God is love and I have come to Ireland to tell you about Him and His son, Jesus. They love you. They love everybody.'

Dichu was impressed by what St Patrick said and gave him his barn. That meant the saint had somewhere to hold church meetings and the barn developed into his first church. (Saul is the Irish for 'barn'.) Dichu didn't become a Christian, although his wife did.

The present church at Saul was built in 1933 and replaced an older one, the ruins of which may be seen in the churchyard. It's beautiful, very simple, in a stunning setting, always open and well worth a visit. It's signposted on the road between Downpatrick and Strangford.

The churchyard contains the ruined remains of an older church and small worn headstones dating back to Celtic times.

Saul Church on the original site of St Patrick's original church.

The original church would have been made of wood and would have looked like an upturned boat. Obviously wooden buildings don't last as long as those made of stone, and even stone ones crumble over time and need to be replaced.

St Patrick lived to be an old man and is thought to have died in Raholp, attended by the clergy of St Tassock's Church. Tradition says his friends couldn't decide where he should be buried. Some thought he should be laid to rest in the church he founded on the Hill of Down, while others favoured his church in Armagh. Eventually they placed his body on a slipe (a primitive cart, without wheels and shaped like a sleigh) and harnessed it to a team of oxen. They agreed that wherever the oxen stopped was where St Patrick should be buried. The oxen stopped near the top of the Hill of Down and he was buried in the grounds of what is now Downpatrick Cathedral. The oral tradition states St Patrick's grave also contains the bodies of St Bridget and St Columba. A large rock was placed on it by Belfast Naturalists' Field Club in 1900.

Down Cathedral, situated on the Hill of Down, is well worth a visit. It contains parts of a Benedictine Monastery, built in 1183. Two small crosses, dating back to the twelfth century, are set into its walls. Building sculpture into walls was once a common practice. It was thought to be a good way to ensure their survival.

The cathedral incorporates the structures of an older church, which had fallen into a terrible state of disrepair and stood, a noble ruin, roofless and derelict, for many years. It was eventually renovated between 1789 and 1812. Today it's a beautiful building with box pews and fine stained-glass windows. Entrance is free and, to help with the upkeep of such an ancient building, it has an unobtrusive, excellent tourist shop.

Churches are not the only places associated with St Patrick. He is said to have blessed many wells throughout the country, including Struell Wells. As well as creating holy wells, St Patrick established major churches in Bangor, Newry, Dromore, and Armagh, and Down Cathedral, which is in Downpatrick and bears his name. His establishment in Bangor became famous for the excellence of the education provided here. It attracted scholars from throughout the then-known world.

St Patrick is said to have planted a yew tree at the land end of Carlingford Lough in Newry, thus giving the city its name, and Armagh developed into the ecclesiastical centre of Ireland. Most of his missionary work was done in the north of Ireland but surprisingly folklore states he never visited the Kingdom of Mourne. He just travelled around the foothills and is said to have looked along the path leading round the shore where the Mountains of Mourne sweep down to the sea, thrown his brogue along it and said, 'May peace reign in their region.' Although St Patrick never visited the Mournes, his followers founded five churches near the shoreline.

St Patrick's main route from Bangor to Armagh was through Downpatrick, Castlewellan, Newry and on to Armagh, but sometimes he travelled from Castlewellan to Seapatrick, Tullylish and on to Armagh. Seapatrick was a convenient place to spend a night, so he founded a church there. Local oral tradition says Seapatrick, now on the outskirts of Banbridge, was founded by the saint himself. It's a long way from the sea, so why is the word 'sea' incorporated in its name?

Words and spellings change over time, so if a word in the past, or a name, bears any resemblance to what we recognise today that's probably what it means. 'Sea' sounds the same as 'See', which is the earliest symbol of a bishop's authority. It usually corresponds to a diocese.

Seapatrick is part of the Diocese of Down and Dromore, one of the two largest dioceses belonging to the Church of Ireland. It stretches from County Down into County Armagh. It contains 477 parishes, 2 cathedrals, (Downpatrick and Armagh), 111 churches,1,800 clergy, 64,500 people and it shares Belfast Cathedral with the Diocese of Conor.

St Patrick's Church at Seapatrick is known locally as the 'wee church' to differentiate it from Banbridge's other Anglican church, Holy Trinity, known as the 'Big Church'. The two churches share clergymen and events.

The wee church has two bells, a small one on a bell tower and a large one at the side. It is the large bell that is tolled manually each Sunday, formerly by the late Rodney Mitchell, who rang the bell weekly for 37 years. It is said a bell has been rung every Sunday on the site since St Patrick walked the earth, except during times of war.

Locally there was great consternation when planning permission was given to build houses adjacent to the site. It was thought that the occupants would object to the sound of the bell. As a result, the leases of the houses state occupants have no right to restrict the sound of a bell that has rung more or less continuously for more than 1,700 years.

St Patrick appears to have been a gentle, affable man but it was possible to make him lose his temper. When Coroticus kidnapped some of his converts, killed the elderly ones and sold the young ones as slaves, he wrote he hoped: 'the riches which he (Coroticus) has unjustly gathered will be vomited from his belly', 'the angel of death will hand him over to be crushed by the anger of dragons', and 'he will be killed with the viper's tongue and an unquenchable fire will consume him'. Stirring words indeed! I must confess when I read them, I warmed to him.

His reaction is very human. Folklore says he got his revenge on Coroticus by turning him into a fox!

St Patrick did a lot of good and was greatly loved and respected. Unfortunately, during the seventh century two monks, Tíerechán and Muirchu, decided to enhance his reputation by writing his life story. Until then St Patrick was a simple sincere man who popularised Christianity.

After Tíerechán and Muirchu had finished with him he passed into folklore, looking more like a wizard, an unbelievable character credited with all sorts of magic powers. For instance, it is said he caused two brothers who were fighting over the ownership of a piece of land to freeze. He told them firmly they wouldn't be able to move unless they gave the land to a church. Another unbelievable tale is that he once asked a dead pagan man why he'd a cross over his grave. The dead man replied it had been put there by mistake. He didn't want it, so St Patrick removed it and set it over the right grave. That was a clever trick because the saint had been dead for several hundred years!

That's the type of story St Patrick's biographers wrote with the intention of enhancing his reputation. Unfortunately they turned him into an unbelievable character and obscured his tremendous achievement. He became the Patron Saint of Ireland and turned what was basically a pagan country into a Christian one. He was a good, simple, sincere man who, despite the dangers of having to work in a hostile environment, laid the foundation of Ireland's reputation as a land of saints and scholars.

SHEELA-NA-GIGS AND JANUS FIGURES

A Sheela-na-gig is the symbol of a strange ancient female figure who clutches her lower regions with a look of agony on her face. She is thought be a fertility figure dating from pagan times and associated with childbirth.

Many pagan symbols were incorporated into Christian beliefs. Christians put water on a baby's head during a christening service because water was regarded as a symbol of wisdom. A wedding ring is a symbol of eternal love because it has no beginning and no end. Celtic knots are composed of many continuous woven threads, usually brightly coloured, each thread representing an individual in a group of people who love each other. Sheela-na-gigs are another example of a Celtic symbol being adapted for Christianity when there was one in every Christian churchyard. Most of the ancient ones were carved from wood. Over time they decayed and disappeared from the landscape, so the only ones left are those carved from stone. Sometimes they have an unusual effect on women. There used to be a history park in County Fermanagh. It was a marvellous place where different types of ancient buildings had been constructed. There was a church constructed from wood. It looked like an upturned boat and had a wooden Sheela-na-gig in its churchyard. I once saw a strange-looking woman catch sight of it, scream 'Mother!', rush towards it, throw her arms around it and burst into tears. Unfortunately the history park was uneconomic, so it disappeared.

Sheela-na-gigs were important figures, so were placed near church doors. There is a Sheela-na-gig on White Island in County Fermanagh. She has a wide mouth, bulging cheeks and was carved in Ulster. She is unusual because her breasts are covered by a cape. Similar figures are found in Killadeas in Fermanagh and Carndonagh in Donegal, so it has been suggested there was once a tradition of stone carving that was restricted to Ulster's western side. There was a taboo recorded in an Ulster saga that forbade men to look at a woman's breasts, so men with exposed breasts were sent out at the front of battle lines so the enemy would avert their eyes!

Janus figures differ from Sheela-na-gigs in that they have a head and a body that is carved on two sides. There are two interesting Janus figures in Cladragh Cemetery on Boa Island. It's on the road to Kesh, approximately 15 miles from Enniskillen. It's a very narrow road, about 5 miles long, and it's not obviously an island because bridges join each end of it to the mainland. These Janus figures are

Janus figure on Boa Island.

Figure in Killadeas churchyard.

easily found because the churchyard is clearly marked off a very minor road that runs directly from the main road. There are two other easily reached Janus figures in Killadeas graveyard, which is near the Manor House Hotel. (Kil, or Cil, means ancient church. Killadeas got its name from the Culdees – Ceile.)

SION MILLS

Sion Mills was established by the Herdman family in 1835. They converted an old flour mill on the River Mourne in County Tyrone into a flax-spinning mill. They had a vision of creating a well-educated, non-sectarian, temperate, moral, God-fearing, contented community. They built a model village with its own school, churches, recreational and sporting facilities. Their cricket team was the village's pride and joy. They believed they were top notch, so challenged the West Indies cricket team to a match in their cricket club during July 1969. The West Indies were on a short visit to England at the time. They had played a test match at Lord's, which was a thrilling match that ended in a draw. They were full of confidence when they crossed the Irish Sea to play against a provincial team in a small village. The match took place on a beautiful day. Sion Mills is a picturesque village. There was a good crowd, the wicket wasn't bad. It was damp and there was a good deal of grass. The West Indies team were full of confidence, which was quickly knocked out of them. In 25 overs the visiting team were out for a score of 25! Members of the local team were ecstatic! That was the lowest ever scored against Ireland, the previous being 29, achieved against New York in 1909. The previous lowest in Ireland was 32, scored by Scotland in 1911. The visiting team excused themselves by saying the pitch was too slow for them as they'd come from fast conditions. If you ask the locals why they won, the more dishonest ones say, 'Johnny Walker was on our side!' Honest locals say, 'They had a good dose of Irish hospitality fuelled by poiteen.'

Mrs Cecil Frances Alexander, the famous hymn writer, lived in a Georgian house in Sion Mills in her girlhood years. During that time she wrote 'All Things Bright and Beautiful'. The 'hill' situated to the east of the village is 'the Purple Headed Mountain' and 'The river running by' is the River Mourne. Cecil caused a scandal in the family when she was 27 by marrying a man six years younger than herself, the Revd William Alexander! That was a terrible thing to do in those days – men were supposed to be older than their wives! However, the age difference didn't worry the young couple in the least. They were very happy together and had four children. William became Bishop of Derry and it was while living there

Cecil wrote 'There is a Green Hill Far Away'. It is thought that 'the green hill far away outside the city wall' was the one she saw in Sion Mills when she looked out of the window while sitting with a very ill child. Her husband eventually became Archbishop of Armagh, the Anglican Church's top job in Ireland, but it was growing up in Sion Mills that inspired her to write hymns. The village has a distinct, quirky, magical personality. The name is an unusual combination of English and Irish. 'Mill' means 'mill', while 'Sion' has two possible meanings, either 'the seat of Finn' the Irish giant, or sidheán (also spelt síodhán or sián), which means 'fairy mound'. Personally, I feel the village is fairy kissed and look upon the second meaning as the correct one.

THE STAR-SPANGLED BANNER

America's national anthem,'The Star-Spangled Banner', is widely credited to John Stafford Smith – but the English composer never claimed credit for writing the original tune itself, leading some to the theory that it was based on an old Irish tune by Turlough O'Carolan (1688–1763), a blind harper who was born in County Meath. He was the son of a farmer. He lost his eyesight when he was 18, so earning a living through farming was impossible. He had a gift for music and for writing poetry, and his parents decided the best thing he could do way to use his talents to make a living. His friend, Dermont Munroe, taught him to play a harp. He was given a horse and some money by another friend, Mrs Munroe, so he set off as an itinerant musician travelling the length and breadth of Ireland. He loved County Fermanagh and spent many happy days there. He was a superb harper who was hired to play in the big houses. When he was working in Tempo Manor he met Mary Maguire, the love of his life. The couple married and had six daughters and one son. He was heartbroken when she died in 1733. He died in 1738.

O'Carolan was a gifted composer as well a superb harpist. I love the names of some of the old Scottish songs he wrote variations on, such as 'Cockup your Beaver'. He wrote many new tunes including 'Planxty Maguire', which was written for O'Cuchonnacht Maguire, the son of Brian Maguire (he swore allegiance to King James I of England after the 'flight of the earls' and was granted 2,000 acres of land around Tempo) and 'Bumper Squire Jones' – the latter possibly the tune that's used for the American National anthem, 'The Star-Spangled Banner'.

O'Carolan's music could have disappeared, along with that of other harpists, if it hadn't been for the work of Edward Bunting (1773–1843), who wrote it down. There's a plaque commemorating him in St George's Church, High Street, Belfast.

T

THE TITANIC QUARTER

The Titanic Quarter in East Belfast around the dock area is dominated by two huge cranes belonging to Belfast's shipyard, Harland and Wolff: Samson and Goliath. Although they are comparative newcomers to the docks (Samson was erected in 1969, Goliath in 1974), they have come to symbolise Belfast in a way that no other building or monument has ever done. Their combined lifting capacity of almost 1,700 tonnes is one of the largest in the world. The Titanic Quarter contains one of the world's top tourist attractions, the Titanic Museum, which celebrates, as the name suggests, the birth of *Titanic*, which was, at the time it was built, the largest, most beautiful, most luxurious ship in the world. She sank on her maiden voyage, a disaster caused by miscommunication, cost cutting and hubris.

Iceberg warnings ignored, the order was given to sail full steam ahead. The ship hit an iceberg, was badly damaged and sank with a record loss of life. More than

Samson and Goliath, Harland and Wolff Shipyard. Where *Titanic* was docked before its ill-fated maiden voyage.

1,500 perished! More people drowned than should have, because there was no regulation at the time for liners to carry sufficient lifeboats for every passenger. The British inquiry held after the disaster was overseen by the Board of Trade. It changed the law so it became mandatory for all ships to pay attention to safety with sufficient lifeboats and lifebelts for every passenger.

Titanic was built in what Belfast people called 'the yard', Harland and Wolff's. It was once the largest single shipyard in the world. I was born in Belfast and like all other natives I was proud of our yard and 'our ships'. We took a great interest in them. During both world wars, ships dominated the skyline of East Belfast. It was badly bombed during the Second World War, but in spite of that produced more ships than any other British shipyard. We knew the name of every ship built, followed it from its conception, through the planning stage, the excitement of employing workers, the ecstasy of the launch and the interesting gossip about the important person who swung the traditional bottle of champagne. I remember as a young child in true, economical, Ulster fashion, asking my grandfather, Sam Finlay, a joiner who had worked on *Titanic*'s first-class cabins, why a bottle of champagne was wasted by being broken on the bow of a ship. If they had to break a bottle, why not use one filled with water? That wouldn't cost anything, and if they wanted something with a bit of fizz what was wrong with lemonade? Grandpa had a hearty laugh before saying:

> The people who launch ships are 'quality folk'. They are so used to having enough to eat and everything else they want, a bottle of water wouldn't mean anything to them. They would have to waste a bottle of the most expensive champagne to get any sort of a kick out of it!

According to Grandpa, *Titanic* had very high-quality workmanship and was really beautiful. That was confirmed when the wreck was found years later. Grandpa said, 'We took a real pride in our work. The Good Lord expects us to do our best at everything we tackle, and we did.' He was chosen to sail on her as part of the guarantee team and was disappointed as he had to refuse because my grandmother was very ill at the time. In later life he said Granny's illness had saved his life. Seven hundred of the crew perished, including all of those from Belfast. They were paid up until the hour the ship sank and there was no compensation.

The Titanic Museum tells the story of the shipyard in the early twentieth century. It's possible to walk on gantries that sway and to travel down in a 'car' through the yard to see men inserting rivets and so on. An impression of the noise and smell is given but neither it, nor the swaying gantry, is strong enough to be unpleasant. Too much realism deters tourists! It's also possible to 'travel' up through the ship from the bottom to the top, visiting the engine room, the cabins, dining rooms and deck and so on, by using projected images and sounds. The Titanic Museum tour finishes with a movie of the discovery of *Titanic* lying on the ocean floor.

Titanic was built by the White Star Line because it was worried by competition from Cunard. Bruce Ismay invited Lord Pirrie, one of the directors of Harland and Wolff, and gave him a contract to build three ships: *Olympic*, *Titanic* and *Gigantic*, which was renamed *Britannic*. *Britannic* was requisitioned for use during the First World War. It was launched in 1915, became the largest hospital ship in the world and was sunk by a mine off the coast of Turkey in 1916.

Lord Pirrie was very unpopular with his workers. He wouldn't allow them to smoke at a time when everyone smoked. If they needed to visit the facilities, they had to sign a stick out and in. If they were away from their workplace for more than seven minutes their pay was docked! There's a story of him meeting a workman who had the sole of his boot gaping away from the upper. Lord Pirrie asked him why his footwear was in such a terrible state and the man replied, 'I have four children and it's very hard to make ends meet. I can't afford new boots.' Lord Pirrie took out his well-filled wallet, removed the thick elastic band holding his bank notes together, handed it to the man and said, 'Here, take this. It should help hold the sole of your boot against the upper!' In true Northern Ireland vernacular Lord Pirrie was described as 'tight as a duck's arse in a hailstorm' and 'so mean he wouldn't give you the steam of his piss'!

The pump house.

The Titanic Museum is very interesting but it is not *Titanic*'s authentic footprint. To see that, go to the Alexandra dry dock and pump house. It's possible to take a guided tour incorporating the dry dock and pump house. The dry dock is where *Titanic* was built and the pump house holds the pumps that removed water from the dock. The pump used to build *Titanic* has been replaced. Climbing down into the dry dock and looking up is awe inspiring! It demonstrates how large the ship was. Incidentally, Belfast gin is manufactured in the repurposed pump house.

During the summer months it's possible to take an hour-long cruise in Belfast harbour and along the River Lagan and view where *Titanic* was built from the water, as well as other attractions such as HMS *Nomadic* (see previous) and HMS *Caroline*.

HMS *Caroline* was launched and commissioned in 1914. She joined the fleet at Scapa Flow in 1916, and is the only ship still in existence that fought in the Battle of Jutland. In 1918 the Admiralty experimented in launching light aircraft from a platform that was built on her. She is the second oldest surviving ship that was commissioned by the Royal Navy, HMS *Victory* being the oldest.

U

U-BOAT AND KILKEEL'S FISHING FLEET

U-boat *UB-64*, commanded by Otto von Schrader, on 30 May 1918 attacked and sank the fleet of Kilkeel's fishing boats some 12 to 15 miles out in the Irish Sea. Not a single life was lost. The then cook boy, Tommy Doonan, who was aboard the *Never Can Tell*, was interviewed in 1974 and has left a record of the event published in *Ulster Commentary*, a magazine once produced by the Northern Ireland Office.

He said:

> We set sail, saw the fishing fleet, joined it and shot our nets. We'd no thought of danger until a U-boat came alongside and we were suddenly looking down the barrel of a machine gun.
>
> The U-boat Commander asked, in English, if we'd had any guns? We shouted, 'No!' and he demanded to speak to our skipper and told him we'd have to abandon ship.
>
> One of the U-boat crew jumped on to the deck of the 'Never Can Tell' clutching either a bomb or a grenade. He knocked it on the boat's rail, threw it into the hold and yelled at us to board the submarine.
>
> When we were all aboard we were told to put our hands above our heads and stand along the conning tower casing. That was scary! If something had frightened the U-boat so it had to submerge we'd have drowned. And I was even more frightened when one of the German sailors smiled at me and touched my head. Was he trying to reassure me, or looking forward to killing me later? The U-boat pulled away and headed in the direction of another Kilkeel boat, the 'Saint Mary'. We heard a muffled 'thump' and saw our wee ship sink beneath the waves.
>
> The Germans repeated the process beside the St Mary, but this time the crew were ordered to take to their punt before their boat was blown up.

> The 'Cyprus', the 'Sparkling Wave', the 'Honey Bee', the 'Lloyds', the 'Jane Gordon' and the 'Marianne McCrum of Annalong' all suffered the same fate. Then the U-boat turned North and sank three boats from the Ardglass fishing fleet. Our spirits went down with every sinking. Our livelihoods were disappearing before our eyes and many of the boats weren't insured.
>
> When the U-boat drew alongside the Moss Rose I thought she was 'for it'. She had an engine but no punt. The Germans put us aboard and told the crew to head for home and stay clear of the overloaded punts rowing towards the shore.

The U-boat commander went out of his way to save the lives of the fishermen, which, at the time, was extremely unusual. Why? One of the Germans asked the fishermen if they knew Mrs Collins of Mountain Road, Kilkeel. Local tradition says a German lad stayed in Mrs Collins' lodging house before the war and he loved the area and its people. Were the fishermen's lives spared because of the hospitality of the Mourne area?

Mary Anne Collins was married to a fisherman, Joseph Collins. He died and she is listed in the 1901 census as running a lodging house on the Mountain Road, so it is possible her kindly behaviour saved the lives of Kilkeel's fishermen during the First World War.

Recent photograph of Kilkeel fishing fleet.

URNEY BELL

The Urney Bell hung in the grounds of St Mary's Church, Strabane. It is huge, more than 8ft in circumference, and is the parishioners' pride and joy. The Urney Bell has an interesting history. It was bought by the Most Revd James Connolly PP at a cost of £72 10*s* 10*d* in 1869 to mark the opening of the Church of St Columba at Doneyloop in the Parish of Urney.

In 1904 the Revd Father John McElhatton was appointed parish priest of Urney. He bought land at Melmont, near Strabane, and built a parochial house beside the church that opened its doors in 1846. When he moved to Melmont he took the Urney Bell with him! He was a very forceful character, and while the parishioners of Urney were very annoyed it was stolen and taken to St Mary's Church in Melmont, Strabane, they did not dare argue with Father John!

When the Second World War began in 1939, the British government became short of metal for armaments so it requisitioned all iron and metal objects for the war effort. Soldiers in the Strabane area, and throughout the Province, began removing wrought-iron gates, fences, balconies, church bells and so on. The parishioners of St Mary's decided they didn't want to sacrifice their bell to the war effort. It was too precious, so one dark night a group of parishioners met in the churchyard and hid the bell by burying it in an inconspicuous position at the back of their graveyard. One of the reasons St Mary's parishioners cared so much for the Urney Bell must have been that they had been insisting for years that it was their bell, they had every right to it! It stayed buried for so many years that nobody could remember where it was!

Eventually a new curate, with an enquiring mind, was appointed to Melmont, He wondered why there was an empty plinth outside his church? He heard the story about the bell and went to look for it. He found a grave that didn't appear to belong to anyone and was marked with the name R. Bell. There was no record of an R. Bell ever having been buried, so he wondered if the Urney Bell was buried in the grave. It was!

The population of St Mary's expanded and a new Church of St Mary's was built in 1970. The Revd Fr Anthony Mulvey was appointed parish priest in 1978. Several years after his appointment he had a new plinth constructed outside the church and the Urney Bell was hoisted into it. It's still there today and the congregation of Doneyloop are still annoyed their bell hangs in the grounds of St Mary's Church, Belmont. But would it have survived the Second World War if it hadn't been stolen? It's an interesting question!

V

VAMPIRE TREE

Folklore states that an evil witch doctor, called Mogh-Dhu, brought his followers to live in Ireland at the place we now know as Rostrevor. They were a bad lot who worshipped demons, murdered people and sucked their blood. Christian missionaries fought and eventually killed all the demon worshippers except Mogh-Dhu. He climbed a young tree and hid by climbing into a small opening. He couldn't get out and died. His tissues and evil blood-sucking habits were absorbed by the tree, which became evil, with lower branches that reached the ground. Birds in the air knew to stay away from it and people learned not to go close because the lower branches curled round them, and Mogh-Dhu's vampire spirit sucked their blood out before throwing their lifeless bodies out on to the ground. Thankfully the evil tree no longer exists. It was blown down by the Big Wind that devastated Ireland on 6 January 1839. Examination of the tree's rings proved that it was many hundreds of years old.

VAN MORRISON

My friend Seamus McCanny, who lives in County Fermanagh, told me Van Morrison wrote 'BrownEyed Girl' on a piano in Derrygonnelly. I was very interested because Van was born in East Belfast in 125 Hyndford Street in August 1945. He was Christened George Ivan Morrison. His father, George Morrison, worked in Harland and Wolff's shipyard as an electrician. His mother, Violet Morrison (née Stitt), was a singer and tap dancer in her youth. He was their only child. Van refused to let the organisation that erects blue plaques put one up on his house but a new owner erected one of their own volition.

The original title of 'Brown Eyed Girl' was 'Brown-Skinned Girl', but Van said he made a mistake and changed the name when he'd finished recording in June 1967. He was 22 years of age when it became his first American top ten single.

It has become a standard that gets frequent airplay, although Van's on record saying, 'I've got about 300 songs I think are better.' It was listed at 109 on the *Rolling Stone* magazine list of 500 Greatest Songs of All Time in November 2004, and was inducted into the Grammy Hall of Fame in 2007.

It would be logical to think that the brown-eyed girl lived in Belfast, especially as Van is on record as saying:

> Belfast is my home. It is where I first heard the music that influenced and inspired me, it is where I first performed and it is somewhere I have referred back to many times in my songwriting over the past 50 years.

He has written songs such as 'On Hyndford Street', 'Cyprus Avenue', 'Orangefield', and so on that refer to places in East Belfast, and it is possible to go on Van Morrison tours around the area. But, and it's a big but, Seamus McCanny is an excellent local historian and he lives in Fermanagh, so I went to Derrygonnelly to see if I could trace the brown-eyed girl. I walked around the village, found the 'The Old Pal's Bar' and thought it looked a likely place, so chose it as a starter. It's the type of place I love, full of character, not gentrified or updated, and it had a helpful barman, Stephen Donaldson.

I asked Stephen if Van Morrison had written 'Brown Eyed Girl' in Derrygonnelly. He replied:

> Yes of course he did. I can't remember the exact year. Early in his solo career he spent several summer months living here with his friend, Gerald Flanagan, in an old unoccupied house near Derrygonnelly on the lower slopes of Knockmore Mountain.
>
> Van was very friendly with a local girl. She was a real beauty, so she was! He sorted out his song on our piano. There's a framed photo of him on the wall at the back. Come on and I'll show you. He said Gerald Flanaghan was his agent.

Stephen showed me the photograph and said, 'I believe that photo was taken by Gerald Flanagan and used on the dust cover of the original recording of 'Brown Eyed Girl'.

According to Stephen, shortly afterwards Van and Gerald went to America and struck up a deal with a record company. The rest is history. 'Brown Eyed Girl' topped the American hit parade. Unfortunately Van and Gerald had some kind of serious disagreement and are no longer friends. As for the identity of the brown-eyed girl? Natives of Derrygonnelly know who she is and Stephen took me across the street to meet her. Unfortunately she was out. Stephen said she's still, after all these years, very attractive.

Van differs from the vast majority of musicians, such as Barry Douglas and James Galway, who were born and bred in Northern Ireland, in that he still lives in the land of his birth.

W

WHITE COWS

Folklore tells the tales of many white cows. Perhaps the most famous is the magic one that came out of Lough Neagh. A monastic church, built by St Colman in AD 590, was being rebuilt because it had been destroyed in 1166. The cow produced so much milk that all the men working on the church's reconstruction had plenty to drink, as well as cheese and butter to eat. The milk was used as building mortar in both the church and in the Celtic cross. It proved very hard to chip. The place got its name when the building was finished and the cow swam out into Lough Neagh, looked back and mooed 'Ardboe'. 'Ard' means height and 'bo' means cow, so 'Ardboe' means 'the height of the cow'.

'Daisy, if ye'd only been a white cow I could have sold ye!'

At that time there were very few cows in Ireland, only sheep. Many people were envious of the magic cow, especially as she was such a good milker, and she was stolen. Luckily there were so few cows her hoofprints were easily identified. She had a calf with her, and every time she put her foot on a flat stone she left a print. Sometimes there was also a print from her calf and a mark left by a stick belonging to the man who had stolen her. The footprints led along the shore to Blackwater in County Armagh and on to Benburb. When she was found she was taken back to Ardboe, where a very close eye was kept on her.

Tradition states that the Celtic cross in Ardboe Church grounds is the oldest in Northern Ireland. It is elaborately carved with Biblical scenes and was erected near the burial ground of babies who were either stillborn or died shortly after birth. Water that gathered at its foot was regarded as holy water and was thought to have healing properties. People came from miles around to collect it. Unfortunately those who were emigrating used to take a hammer and chisel to knock a bit off the cross to take with them and bring them luck. The district council put railings around it to keep that from happening.

The churchyard itself is interesting because it contains a mark on a stone said to be a depression caused by St Patrick's knee when he knelt there in the fifth century. The graves in the churchyard are unusual because the women buried there reverted to their maiden name after death. There's a headstone that says, 'Sacred to the memory of Peggy Devlin, spouse of Dominick O'Farrell who departed this life on the sixteenth of August seventeen twenty'. Another is engraved with the names of Bernard Lappin, who died in 1712, and his wife Grace Kelly, who died in 1727.

X

XENOPHOBIA

Xenophobia may be defined as having attitudes and prejudices that reject people because they are thought to be a threat, or are outsiders to the community or a danger to national identity. After the outbreak of the Second World War, the authorities believed that German nationals living in Northern Ireland could be spies, so after 3 September 1939 they were interned in a prisoner-of-war camp near Gilford, County Down. Some of the old Nissen huts used to accommodate them are still standing about a mile from the village on the left-hand side of the road when travelling from Gilford to Lurgan.

Some time ago I met Miss Grosse, who was born in Germany before the war and became a teacher in Grosvenor High School, Belfast. She was a lovely gentle lady and she told me she had come to Northern Ireland before the war to be immersed in English as part of her degree course. As a result she was arrested, processed and locked up in a prisoner-of-war camp on the outskirts of Gilford for the duration. I was horrified! Imagine suspecting such a nice person like her could be a German spy! When I told her my thoughts, she laughed and said:

> Being in that prisoner of war camp was one of the nicest things that ever happened me. Northern Ireland's government is crazy, but ordinary people are very kindly. They understand the law, but if it strikes them as being stupid, they ignore it. Our guards quickly decided we were harmless. We had good craic with them and the Gilford people felt sorry for us. We were in the middle of rich farming land and thanks to the generosity of the locals I was much better fed than if I had been stuck in Belfast existing on the meagre rations legally due to me. Every day we were given fresh farm produce, eggs, cream butter, home-baked cakes and so on. At night our guards bade us 'goodnight' and locked us up. The fence surrounding the internment camp looked secure, but there was a place at the back where we could lift the wire and get out. It was an easy walk into Gilford. We went into the local pubs, made friends and went visiting. I couldn't imagine anywhere apart from Ireland where you could

> escape from prison, go into a pub and be bought a drink by your prison guard. We had a good night out before crawling back into prison. We were having such a good time the last thing anyone wanted to do was escape. In fact, when the war ended and we were repatriated we burst into tears and pleaded, to no avail, to be allowed to stay in Northern Ireland. We had to go back home to Germany. The first thing we did on arriving back in Germany was buy a one-way ticket back to Northern Ireland and I am now a British citizen!

Miss Grosse loved Northern Ireland and never went back to Germany! She was lucky. The government's xenophobia worked to her advantage!

Another example of xenophobia occurred when Sunderland flying boat NJ186 from 423 Squadron, Royal Canadian Air Force, which was based at Castle Archdale in County Fermanagh, left on Sunday, 20 May 1945, to look for U-boats the authorities thought might make a dash for freedom through the Irish Sea. Flight Lieutenant Washington, the navigator on board the Sunderland, recorded:

> The weather was foul. Castle Archdale was surrounded in dense fog. Our motto was that we flew when seagulls walked! At precisely 0700 hours we became airborne, loaded with 2,200 gallons of fuel, a ton of depth charges and full load of ammunition. Our Sunderland had recently been equipped with an early-model radar, which appeared to identify physical landmarks appropriate to our intended track. We marvelled at this amazing invention, which could render dead-reckoning navigation obsolete, I went to the flight deck and, standing between the 1st and 2nd pilots (Flight Lieutenant Gerry Allen and Flight Lieutenant 'Ole' Olsen), I said, 'We have crossed Ireland and you can now descend over the Irish Sea.' Instead of descending in normal fashion, our captain, in a moment of playfulness or exasperation, nosed down and we were in rapid descent. I had just finished saying, 'For Christ's sake Gerry, you don't have to play dive bomber' when I saw solid land ahead. At the same instant, I saw the 2nd pilot's left forearm push all four throttles full ahead to the fire wall and his right hand pulled back on the control column. A split second later, we lurched and slowed perceptibly and there appeared in front of the 'boat' an orange flash which blotted out all else. In addition to the surge in engine power, I heard a terrible grinding, crunching sound. The Sunderland was about 12 miles south of its intended track, and had struck the summit of Slieve Fadda near Rostrevor. Miraculously, it was still flying and only one member of the crew had been slightly injured. An inspection revealed that the bottom of the hull was ripped away together with the galley containing stove, table

> and benches. The starboard float, aileron and wing tip were gone, the radar, radio and electrical systems were seriously damaged and the air speed indicator was unserviceable. In addition, a crack several millimetres wide had developed at the fuselage/starboard wing junction. Fortuitously, the solid fog opened, revealing Jurby airfield on the north-west of Isle of Man. Our pilot, Gerry Allen, managed to crash-land the boat on one runway, in blatant disregard of an instruction from the control tower operator to use an alternative location and in spite of being threatened with a court martial!

The crash landing caused further damage and a fire, but the crew managed to escape before the Sunderland exploded. Xenophobia caused them to be arrested and imprisoned until their identities had been confirmed and it was obvious they weren't German spies!

Y

YEATS FAMILY

Revd William Butler Yeats, Rector of Tullylish Anglican Church, County Down, from 1834 to 1862 raised an extremely talented family. His son, John, became a well-known artist and the father of both the author William Butler Yeats (1865–1939) and the artist Jack Butler Yeats (1871–1939).

The Revd Yeats was Rector of Tullylish during the Great Famine (1845–48). His parishioners weren't impressed when he first arrived because all they knew about him was that he was an expert horseman. They complained, 'We asked for a preacher not a bloody horseman.' They quickly warmed to him because he was a compassionate man who felt the plight of his parishioners keenly and decided to do something about it. He proved to be a charismatic preacher. This ability, combined with his expertise as a horseman, proved invaluable during the famine. His parishioners were dying of starvation and he helped them by riding around Ireland preaching and using the money he earned to buy food. He, like the majority of Victorians, did not believe people should be given something for nothing. They believed that would encourage laziness, so he sold food at highly subsidised rates. If a family in his parish was so poverty stricken they couldn't afford his very reasonable prices, he didn't let them starve. He helped them in spite of his ingrained belief that goods should be earned. As well as collecting money, he wrote to the then Prime Minister, John Russell (1792–1878), and pleaded for help to be given to the starving Irish.

His son, John Butler Yeats, gained an excellent reputation as an artist, while his grandchildren had spectacular careers. In 1923 the Nobel Prize for Literature was awarded to his grandson, William Butler Yeats, who became one of the foremost figures of twentieth-century literature (see previous), a driving force behind the Irish Literary Revival who was involved in the establishment of Dublin's Abbey Theatre. His brother, the artist Jack Yeats, received many awards, including honorary degrees from universities such as the University of Ireland, Trinity

'Maybe we should all become expert horsemen?'

College Dublin and so on, and also the French Legion of Honour. The origins of these extraordinary talents developed through the lineage of a preacher in the tiny, peaceful, sleepy village of Tullylish, in County Down.

YELLOW MAN

Yellow man is a sweet that today is rarely on sale in Northern Ireland except at the Auld Lammas Fair in Ballycastle. No visit to Ballycastle is complete without eating yellow man, which is usually accompanied by dulse, a seaweed that grows at low tide. They have been immortalised in the words of a traditional song:

> Did you treat your Mary Ann
> To some dulse and yellow man.
> At the Auld Lammas Fair in Ballycastle-O

Yellow man is like a dense honeycomb. It's made from brown sugar, golden syrup, butter, vinegar, and baking soda (some recipes vary slightly).

The Auld Lammas Fair is Ireland's oldest fair. The word Lammas originates from Lughnasadh, an ancient Celtic festival celebrating the beginning of the harvest season. It takes its name from the sun god, Lugh, father of Cucuhlaine, the Hound of Ulster in Celtic mythology.

Z

ZOO

Belfast Zoo was opened in 1934 on the side of Cave Hill. It's in a spectacular location overlooking Belfast Lough. It co-operates with worldwide zoos conserving animals that are going extinct in the wild, and at present is home to more than 500 animals. It was the first zoo in the UK and Ireland to successfully breed Goodfellow's tree-kangaroo and is currently home to Jaya and Hasu-Hasu, a breeding pair. Specialised zookeepers are responsible for cleaning, feeding, enrichment, record keeping, observing behaviour, as well as environmental and enclosure work and visitor interactions. Sometimes zookeepers have to hand-rear animals and are particularly proud of having hand-reared Lily, the Barbary lion cub. The zoo vet looks after the animals' health.

The zoo champions local wildlife. It provides a sanctuary for rescued or injured hedgehogs, has installed swift nest boxes and a swift sound box. It has funded chough research in partnership with Dublin Zoo and Fota Wildlife Park, played an active role in the red squirrel breeding programme, funded barn owl research for Bird Watch Ireland and has provided a sanctuary for two rescued barn owls, which visitors can see in the zoo's farm. It hosts regular events for the Northern Ireland Bat Group and has participated in native species events for a range of organisations, as well as developing on-site wildflower meadows.

Belfast, like other British cities, was blitzed during the Second World War. It suffered its first blitz on 7–8 April 1941, when Harland and Wolff's shipyard was devastated. Although the zoo wasn't harmed, the authorities felt if it was bombed dangerous animals could escape and attack members of the public. As a result, thirty-three animals including racoons, six wolves, a puma, two polar bears, a black bear, a hyena, a tiger, a lynx and a vulture were shot. One of the monkeys must have felt that was no fun so it escaped and ended up in the cot of my brother-in-law, Alan Finlay. His father, Major James St Clair Finlay, was away fighting in the war. They lived on the Whitewell Road, in Belfast, near the zoo. On the day in question, Alan's mother, Molly Finlay, put him down to sleep. Sometime later she heard him gurgling, went to pick him up and discovered there

Monkey in Belfast Zoo.

was a monkey in his cot and he was chatting to it. It must have climbed up the drainpipe and in through the open window. Molly was one of the few people to have a phone, so she rang the zoo and a keeper came and collected it. It's a family joke that she gave the wrong monkey back!

The authorities decided elephants weren't dangerous, so they survived. Sheila was a baby Asian elephant and her keeper, Denise Austin, loved her and thought she'd be frightened during the Blitz so she brought the baby elephant home with her every night to sleep in her garage. Denise was the zoo's first woman keeper. She lived in 278 Whitwell Road, a typical small semi-detached house, with her mother, Irene Beatrice Mary Austin. She had a small garden and a garage and it was one of the last places you'd think of housing an elephant! Denise's relatives had a farm and gave her bales of hay, so the baby elephant had better-quality food than was available in the zoo.

The Whitewell Road is near the zoo, curving from the Antrim Road down to the Shore Road. Denise waited each day until the zoo was closed, then quietly led Sheila out of her enclosure and down the road to her house. Local residents were very supportive. Sometimes Denise and Sheila stopped at the Thrones Stores, where the owner gave Denise stale bread while Sheila helped herself to cabbages and other goodies displayed outside. Apparently an old woman, who had never seen an elephant before, went into the local police station and said, 'I saw the strangest animal outside Thrones Stores. It had a tail at both ends. It was stealing cabbages with one of its tails, and if I told you what it was doing with them you'd never believe me!' I've no idea if that's true or not, but it's the kind of tale you couldn't make up!

Sheila and Denise were very contented until one evening a dog barked at them. Sheila took umbrage, pulled her lead out of Denise's hands, chased the dog to the house where it lived and broke down the picket fence surrounding the garden. Its owner complained and the head zookeeper, Dick Foster, hauled Denise over the coals. Denise was told she must never take Sheila home again. She agreed and left Sheila in the zoo, but whenever the siren warned of a possible air attack she ran back to the zoo and spent the night with the little elephant, comforting her by rubbing her ears.

Denise and Sheila's story has been fictionalised on many occasions and turned into theatre plays and movies. Michael Morpurgo, the former children's laureate and author of *Warhorse*, wrote *An Elephant in the Garden* (published by Harper Collins children's books) based on Sheila's story but he set the story in Dresden Zoo. I feel disappointed the story has been fictionalised. Surely the plain truth is sufficient. I can't think of anything more stirring than the thought of a lone woman hugging a baby elephant during the war with the sight and sound of bombs falling and lighting up the sky. Denise became known as 'the elephant angel'.

Belfast Zoo's first elephant was called Daisy. She arrived the day before the zoo was opened to the public on 27 March 1934. She crossed the Irish Sea on the Heysham steamship. A zoo worker, Manus Kane, was sent to meet her. He hadn't a baldy notion about how she should be handled and was grateful to see a hooked stick hanging from her ear, with a message reading 'Lead me with this'. He held the stick out, Daisy wrapped her trunk around it and followed him. The sight of an elephant scared a baker's carthorse. It bolted down York Street, scattering loaves all over the place. Daisy ate the bread and decided she needed a second course. She spied a fruit and vegetable display in a greengrocer's shop, ran towards it, plundered the display and came out with a big turnip.

There was a cast-iron trough used for watering cart horses outside Shaftesbury Inn on the Antrim Road near the zoo. When Daisy smelt water she decided to have a long drink, before cooling her front feet by putting them in the trough, then squashing her back feet in as well. She sat there for a while washing herself and anyone who came close to her, before completing her approximately 6-mile walk to the zoo.

In 1972, Peter the polar bear disappeared from the zoo in mysterious circumstances. Thanks to my friend, the late Dr David Erwin, I know exactly what happened. David was curator of zoology in the Ulster Museum in Belfast. One day he received a phone call from the zoo asking him if he could stuff a polar bear. He replied, 'I don't have the necessary skill but I know a taxidermist who might take on the job. Why am I being asked such an unusual question?' The zoo keeper replied:

> We're co-operating with a worldwide conservation exercise to breed polar bears. Our male bear, Peter, is now in his twenties and the poor old soul's past it. He's completely useless as far as breeding is concerned so we've acquired a young male bear who is full of enthusiasm for the job. The trouble is, old Peter objects to him! We've had to keep the two bears apart and that's not a feasible long-term solution. It's unkind to keep poor Peter in solitary confinement! We've tried very hard to get him a new home but sadly nobody wants a disagreeable, ancient, impotent polar bear and we decided the best thing we can do is put him to sleep. He's a magnificent specimen. It's an awful pity to waste him so we thought you might like to add him to your collection.

David contacted the taxidermist, who said he's never stuffed such a large animal, but would do his best provided he could watch it moving and take photographs of it. That was agreed and the pair set off in a large van to the zoo. The taxidermist watched Peter move around for some time, took a lot of photographs and eventually said he was ready to do the job. A vet was called and blew a dart into Peter. He said it contained enough sedative to kill ten elephants. Peter continued to walk up and down, so the vet repeated the dose. Peter continued to walk for a few

'It was a shame we had to put Peter to sleep, but there was no kind alternative.'

minutes, then lay down in the corner and started to snore. He was observed for some time. It was getting very late, and the vet said that although Peter still seemed asleep, he was unconscious, would die shortly and it was perfectly safe to load him into the van. David said he was absolutely terrified helping to load snoring Peter into the van and they set off down the Antrim Road. When they reached Cliftonville Circus, they were spotted by an army patrol who noticed the van was carrying a heavy weight. The year was 1972, right in the middle of the Troubles, and heavy loads in vehicles suggested a gang of terrorists carrying a bomb. The army stopped David and asked him what he had in his van. David replied, 'A polar bear!' The soldiers didn't believe him, dragged David and his passenger out of the van, made them stand with their hands above their heads against the side of it and frisked them. They didn't find anything suspicious so they decided to open the van. David suggested that was an unwise thing to do and the soldiers swore at them for telling such an unlikely story! The van was opened, Peter let a big snore, the door was hastily slammed shut and David said he'd never heard such a stream of bad language, ending with, 'They really do have a f***ing polar bear in the f***ing van!' They were allowed to resume their journey. Peter arrived in the museum, died peacefully and was successfully stuffed. He's now a prize specimen. It was a shame to have to put such a beautiful animal to sleep but, in the circumstances, there really was no other option. It's unkind to keep an animal in solitary confinement.

Bibliography

Bates, Nora, *Up the Down Street*, Adare Press, 1994

Campbell, Aidan, *Knock – An Illustrated and Spoken History of Knock, East Belfast,* private publication, printed by Priory Press, Holywood, County Down, March 2008

Killen, John, *A History of the Linen Hall Library 1788–1988*, Linen Hall Library, 1990

Maginnis, Matt, *Mourne Men & the U-Boats 1914–1918*, Blackstaff Press, 2017

McBride, Doreen, *The Little Book of Fermanagh*, The History Press Ireland, 2018

McBride, Doreen, *Tyrone Folk Tales*, The History Press Ireland, 2016

McBride, Doreen and Bell, Jonathan, *Ulster Folk and Farming an Activity Pack*, The Ulster Folk and Transport Museum

McBride, Doreen, *A Little Book of County Down*, The History Press, 2022

Ulster Commentary Magazine, The Northern Ireland Office, 1974

O'Dolan, Mairéad, *The Church Ruins and Stone Monuments Near the Holy Well Belcoo*, private publication, Onedigital, Brighton, 2006

Proudfoot, Lindsay, *Down History and Society*, Geography Publications, Dublin, 1977

Rolston, William and Day Angélique (eds), *Cultivating a Love for Knowledge Two Hundred Years of the Belfast Natural History and Philosophical Society 1821–2021*, Belfast Natural History and Philosophical Society, 2023

Skuce, Dolly, *From Magic Lanterns to Moon Landings*, Adare Press, 1995

Yeats W.B. (ed.), *Irish Fairy and Folk Tales*, London: Walter Scott Ltd